when you love someone in recovery

"... it is one day, one step, and one hug at a time."—Laurie

"... it nourishes the soul in a multitude of ways."—Terry

"... you can all heal."—Jen

"... treat them like a person and not something that's broken."—Kristi

"... though at times you want to give up on them, that's when they need you to hold out hope the most!"—Lori

"... it will take a lot of time for the brain, body, and spirit to find their way."—Annette

"... you learn about acceptance and that you don't have to always like the person you love."—Terri

"... you celebrate the small wins."—Leslie

"... you grieve who they were, fight for who they're becoming, and love them fiercely through both."—Stephanie

when you love someone in recovery

a hopeful guide to understanding addiction

when you love someone in recovery

Caroline Beidler, MSW

An Imprint of Thomas Nelson

When You Love Someone in Recovery

Published by Nelson Books, an imprint of Thomas Nelson, 501 Nelson Place, Nashville, TN 37214, USA. Nelson Books and Thomas Nelson are registered trademarks of HarperCollins Christian Publishing, Inc.

Published in association with The Bindery Agency, www.TheBinderyAgency.com.

Thomas Nelson titles may be purchased in bulk for educational, business, fundraising, or sales promotional use. For information, please email SpecialMarkets@ThomasNelson.com.

HarperCollins Publishers, Macken House, 39/40 Mayor Street Upper, Dublin 1, D01 C9W8, Ireland (https://www.harpercollins.com)

Library of Congress Cataloging-in-Publication Data

Names: Beidler, Caroline, 1982- author

Title: When you love someone in recovery: a hopeful guide to understanding addiction / Caroline Beidler MSW.

Description: Nashville, TN, USA : Nelson Books, [2026] | Summary: "Author, speaker, and addiction recovery expert Caroline Beidler offers friends and family members the gift of being able to understand the recovery lifestyle--a way of life that goes beyond anonymous meetings in church basements and fosters a sense of well-being, healthy coping strategies, discovering new passions, and nurturing a deep personal faith"-- Provided by publisher.

Identifiers: LCCN 2025037831 (print) | LCCN 2025037832 (ebook) | ISBN 9781400253975 trade paperback | ISBN 9781400254132 ebook

Subjects: LCSH: Addicts--Religious life | Recovering addicts--Religious life | Habit breaking--Religious aspects--Christianity

Classification: LCC BV4596.A24 B453 2026 (print) | LCC BV4596.A24 (ebook)

LC record available at https://lccn.loc.gov/2025037831

LC ebook record available at https://lccn.loc.gov/2025037832

Art direction: Curt Diepenhorst
Cover design: Studio Gearbox
Interior design: Kristy Edwards

Printed in the United States of America

26 27 28 29 30 LBC 5 4 3 2 1

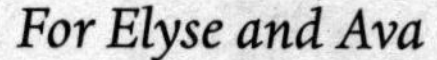

For Elyse and Ava

Contents

Foreword

When I first met Caroline Beidler in person at a recovery conference in Ohio, I had no idea she lived twenty minutes from me in Tennessee. I had only known her through an email friendship we'd struck up, since she was a staffer at the Association of Recovery in Higher Education (ARHE) at the time. ARHE is an organization that supports college students in recovery, and I was doing advocacy work on its behalf.

I didn't know, but would later learn, that as a graduate student she created her university's first recovery community in Madison, Wisconsin.

I didn't know she founded a recovery residence for young women.

I didn't know she started a statewide and nationally recognized recovery coaching program that brings recovery coaches into emergency departments and a nonprofit that empowers other women leaders in recovery.

I didn't know she was a writer, like me.

Over coffee at a nearby coffee shop I learned these things and got acquainted with her generous heart of service for those struggling with substance misuse, having lived the nightmares and traumas of addiction herself.

In this, the third of her remarkable recovery books, she shares four principles of recovery—hope, wellness, community, and service. What strikes me in each of her three books is her prophetic advocacy for communities of safety. Traumas make us feel unsafe. Our nuclear families can make us feel unsafe. Challenges—whether physical, emotional, or spiritual—can make us feel unsafe.

When we feel unsafe, we feel very much alone.

Whether you are in recovery or not, our world today suffers from a crisis of loneliness. As a young woman in her early twenties, Caroline began the work of uniting all of us through creating communities of safety, so we wouldn't feel the heartbreak of loneliness and could heal together.

Today, I hope you have places to go so you are not alone. Some of these might include churches and faith-based groups, recovery homes and community centers, youth organizations and ministries, and of course, recovery groups. There is, however, another place you can go and not leave your home. You can dive into one of Caroline's books. There you will meet a writer who is compassionate and wise beyond her years. Who understands you and the challenges and joys of living a sober life. A contemporary wisdom teacher for our time and someone I feel honored to call my friend today.

Susan Packard
Cofounder of HGTV, author of several books including *The Little Book of College Sobriety*, and woman in long-term recovery

Introduction

When the Light Comes Back

They get dropped off by a friend and you are bracing yourself for the awkward ask for money, the excuses. The way they can't look you in the eyes anymore. The way clothes hang off their body three sizes too big.

You are supposed to meet them for coffee, but you've been down this road before: Broken promises. Hurt. Lies. Fear.

But as you look toward the window, a car pulls up. The passenger door opens.

They approach and you notice right away: Something is different.

They smile. Reach for an embrace. Hold on tight. Tears come. Tears that have been waiting.

Then they look at you and you can't believe it.

Their eyes shine.

Bright.

As if illuminated by stage lights.

The light is back.

Perhaps you have experienced this too. You haven't seen your family member for a while but heard they are in recovery. They went to treatment. Maybe they are living in recovery housing or volunteering in their church's recovery ministry. Maybe they sponsor other folks or go to meetings regularly. You aren't quite sure what it all means, but you know something is different.

Something has happened; something *is happening*.

They are different.

They are new.

When you recognize that your loved one is shining from the inside out, you know that something has changed.

This something, dear reader, is recovery.

As poet Maya Angelou once shared, "Nothing can dim the light that shines from within." This I've found to be especially true in rooms of recovery. Family members and loved ones often have the same description of the person who has entered addiction recovery and started on the healing journey: "The light in their eyes is back."

The Recovery Road

This journey we are about to go on together will illuminate the recovery road for you. Not just addiction (though it is fundamental that we understand this, too, as you'll see in a bit), but recovery. You will learn how the brain heals, how our loved ones can change, and most importantly that recovery is so much more than going to meetings in dark church basements. Recovery is more than sobriety. Recovery is a way of life that shines bright in the world. Something our world needs desperately right now.

Recovery is also something that we can do together.

Maybe you've picked up this book because you have a son, daughter, wife, husband, neighbor, coworker, parent, or pastor in recovery and you want to understand what this means. How can you support and love them? Do you need to be careful with your own alcohol or substance use around them? What do they do to support themselves? What warning signs do you need to be on the lookout for? Are there ways to help your loved one stay on track?

Maybe you picked up this book because you desperately want your loved one to understand. *You* are in recovery. What was once darkness is now like the dawn: A new world is opening before you, and you yearn for your loved one to know what recovery is, what it means to you, and how you've changed.

You want them to experience this new world *with* you.

You long for them to believe in you and trust that no matter what happens, you've changed.

You want them to be excited, not afraid.

Hopeful, not ready for the sky to drop.

Trusting, even if you've been hard to trust in the past or made mistakes.

You've tasted and seen a better way and you can't keep it to yourself.

However you are showing up, whether as a person who identifies with being in recovery or someone who loves us, in these pages you are going to discover what it means to be in recovery—or on your way there.

What to Expect

Almost every family in the world is impacted by addiction. My hope is that soon almost every family in the world will experience and understand what it means to be in recovery. Much of my work as an author, speaker, editor, and consultant working with federal agencies and international partners is to distill what we know about our experiences of recovery into information that is simple to understand and easy to share. Not just so those of us in recovery can understand it better but so our loved ones, family members, and communities can understand what addiction is and how to support us.

Part 1: What Is Recovery? The first part of the book is at the center of everything that follows. Before we build a better understanding of what recovery is and how we can support our loved ones, we need to understand the concepts, definitions, and a bit more about the science. The pillars of recovery that follow all rest on this solid foundation of what recovery is from the perspective of neuroscience, personal experience, recovery pathways, and types of support.

Part 2: Recovery Is Hope. Here I will introduce the first pillar of recovery: the concept of hope, which is a cornerstone of the recovery process. Hope is when we believe that our loved ones can heal and transform after a life of active addiction. Research shows that when family members believe in and have hope for their loved ones, they are more likely to maintain recovery (how amazing is this?!). We also dive deeper into explaining barriers to support, such as stigma, along with understanding the neuroscience of addiction to help counter these barriers. Ultimately, we lay the necessary foundation for family members to understand the process of addiction and the multiple pathways of recovery.

Part 3: Recovery Is Wellness. I will outline how recovery is about more than abstaining from using substances or compulsive behaviors. Recovery is also about physical, emotional, and spiritual health. Those of us in recovery often discover that taking care of our physical health not only helps our bodies but it helps our minds too. I know many a person in recovery who is physically fit, active, and healthy. There are more than a few bodybuilders who are former substance users. But wellness is more than physical health; it's a process that includes mental and spiritual health as well.

Part 4: Recovery Is Community. The recovery journey is more than an individualized one. It happens in church basements in circles of chairs, and it also happens in city centers, college campuses, and church sanctuaries. Today many recovery advocates (including me) are sharing their recovery stories openly and publicly. Research shows that when we share openly, more people reach out for help in their own lives. Sharing recovery allows this process to reach beyond the individual healing journey and into the family, neighborhood, church pew, and city council meeting. Recovery happens in a community of people. For friends and family members, community can be key to understanding and supporting our loved ones.

Part 5: Recovery Is Service. I will close by exploring how purpose is central to recovery. One of the most impactful ways families can support their loved ones is to show through encouragement and support that their lives have purpose and value. Many of us become purpose driven in recovery, and this is evident when family members look at how we spend our time and the ways we are involved in our communities through volunteerism, creating organizations, sharing our stories, starting recovery ministries, or even writing books.

Throughout our journey together, I also include stories and insights from family members—people who have walked the road of addiction recovery themselves and with their loved ones. I'm a firm believer that we learn from the personal experience and stories of others. That's also why I want to hear from you about your experience (learn how to connect with me at the back of the book).

Also at the back of the book are a glossary, exercises, and other helpful resources lovingly cultivated to support you, and all grounded in evidence-based research.

I am so grateful that my husband decided to stick around and learn more about recovery. I'm so honored that my own family, my children included, is committed to understanding and fully supporting my journey. I hope you will stick around to learn more too.

Recovery is an amazing process with countless benefits—not just for the individual themselves, but for the entire family, the community, and all of us.

Are you ready to increase your understanding and learn how to support your loved one who is in or seeking recovery? Let's get to it.

Remember

To help support loved ones, family members need to learn what addiction recovery is and why it matters.

Reflect

What comes to mind when you think of someone who is in addiction recovery?

PART 1

what is recovery?

Chapter 1

Everyone Has a Story

Every great love starts with a great story.
—Nicholas Sparks

I recently asked my husband this question: "When we met, did you know anything about recovery?"

He looked a little sheepish. "I had no clue. I remember stalking you a little on social media when we first started dating. I saw a picture of you wearing a shirt that said Sober Saturday Nights."

I laughed, remembering the shirt. The time (before kids). The blunt black bangs.

"I hate to admit it now, honey, but I was confused. Sober? Saturday nights? My first thought was, *I don't think this is going to work*. I had no idea what recovery was all about. Not like I do now. I had no idea that it makes life bigger, not smaller."

The first time I told him that I couldn't hang out because I was going to a meeting, he was baffled again.

"Meeting? What kind of meeting? Like AA?"

For him, there was only one brand of recovery, and that brand had firmly embedded images of white men in suits with cigs circa 1945, meeting in secretive church basements. They all introduced themselves the same way:

"Hi, my name is Bill and I'm an . . ."

"Hi, Bill."

Later, after we'd been dating for a while and he met my friends in recovery, he was shocked that people "like me" and "us" were a part of this seemingly elusive club where we drank fancy seltzer, laughed a lot, and were sober on Saturday nights, God forbid.

"Wait, Evan the MIT graduate and computer genius? Charles, the lawyer and family man? Shelly the yoga instructor? Are *in recovery*?"

Over the years, my husband has come to understand the fullness of the addiction recovery journey. In our home, recovery is not only a part of my life but a part of our family's. Mine. His. Our children. Even our extended family. It is a way of life that I've shared over time, and it has become a part of the foundation of our daily lives.

My husband's questions early on—and later my children's—have led me to explore this more deeply: *What is recovery?*

We may understand what it means for us, but how can we describe it to the people that we love?

Some define recovery as "a process of change through which individuals improve their health and wellness, live a self-directed life, and strive to reach their full potential."[1]

I love this definition.

Nowhere do we see the words "sober" or "sobriety." Nowhere do we see an emphasis on a set of rules someone has to follow. Recovery is a process and it's about change. It's more than abstaining from problematic substance use; it's about improving health and wellness. It's about finding our people and serving in our communities.

When our loved one finds recovery, the light comes back. And what's more (and amazing) is that research shows that when we have families and friends who support our recovery (even one person), we are more likely to stay the course compared to those who have no one who believes in them.[2]

Maybe you don't identify with the concept of recovery or your loved one is still struggling in active addiction or problematic substance use. Or maybe you are *very* familiar with recovery and have been working in an organization or ministry for years. Maybe you want a resource to share with those you minister to and support. I hope this book is welcome and gets shared like a big hug.

I've been involved in building an international alliance of researchers, experts, peers, and advocacy organizations who have a common mission and vision for increased family recovery support and family recovery research around the world.[3] Recovery, as you will come to see, is a family affair. It impacts every part of the family system and must be included when we talk about policy and programs and advocacy. But it is not just something to be discussed in global gatherings or classrooms.

The issue of family recovery impacts our lives in our central places, in the heart of the home, in the beating hearts of our families. Around kitchen tables and in living rooms. On front porch swings and while shooting hoops in the driveway. In church sanctuaries and in town halls. It impacts us no matter how we define family—whether biological or chosen. The people we are born with or the people we choose to have in our lives.

Every individual and every family has a story to share.

Stories of Recovery

Stories are commonplace in rooms of recovery. We share our struggles with addiction and our experiences with hardships like divorce, grief, pregnancy, infant loss, and relationships. Yet, we also celebrate the bright spots like new ideas, employment opportunities, hopes, dreams, and more. Sharing our stories is not just about disclosing what we've been through or done. It's also about highlighting what it looks like to live a life of second, third, and fourth chances. Not just for our own sakes, but for others.

Each story isn't just a message about where we've been. It's an opportunity to show where we can go together.

As author and advocate Ryan Hampton says, "Sometimes just the message that we do recover is enough to get someone started on the right road."[4]

Holy moments happen when our stories speak to each other. When they reflect the hope that change is possible. When they invite us, in a new way, to look at our experiences with gratitude and even expectation.

I'd like to invite you into the circle and share a piece of William Cope Moyers's story—in his own words—because it's important to show you, at the start of this journey, what is possible. No matter how hopeless your current situation feels as an affected family member. No matter how much sleep you may have lost over a loved one. No matter how much Google searching or ChatGPT-ing you've done trying to find answers.

William's Story

Growing up with parents who were successful journalists, I was part of many conversations around the table at mealtime that included politics, the war in Vietnam, faith, and academic achievement. We didn't talk much about the dangers of alcohol and other drugs. Mostly because my parents didn't think that was a real concern in our household.

Decades later as parents ourselves, my wife and I didn't have a choice when it came to our three children.

She and I met in treatment for our addiction. I worked at Hazelden. On occasion we took our kids to recovery meetings. We never served alcohol in the home because we didn't drink, and so our kids witnessed how it was possible to enjoy holidays and special occasions without being under the influence. I also wrote books about addiction and spoke publicly about my story. When it came to alcoholism and drug dependence, the Moyers family didn't have any secrets.

But we were no dummies either. We told our kids that as the product of two parents in recovery, they were genetically vulnerable and at a higher risk for substance-use problems than their classmates at school or friends in the community. If they chose to drink or take drugs, they might not have the power of choice when it came to the outcome of their decision.

"Maybe you suffer no consequences, or maybe you suffer the same consequences that your parents endured," I often reminded them. And they nodded that they understood the risks.

Still, I wasn't satisfied that all the information and the way their mother and I lived would prove enough to shield them from temptation. That's why I decided to incentivize our two sons and daughter not to experiment.

"If you wait until you're twenty-one, I promise to buy you a new car," I told each of them separately. I explained that the brain, where risk is weighed and choices are made, is the last organ in their young bodies to develop, and if they gave their brains a chance to mature without the influence of substances, it would be to their benefit. They might even avoid addiction altogether the longer they were substance-free. Again, they nodded that they understood the stakes. They seemed excited by the prospect of shiny new wheels!

I never had to make good on my promise to buy them a car. To my shock, all three of them chose to drink or take drugs or both before they reached their twenty-first birthdays. All three of them developed serious challenges with mood and mind-altering substances.

Thank goodness my wife and I gave them one more tool in the toolbox of information, practical experience, and unconditional love to empower them in dealing with these challenges. "If you get tangled up with substances, it is okay to come to us and ask for help," we assured our kids. "There is nothing wrong with asking for help."

One of our sons was in college when he came home for the holidays and confided, "Dad, I've stopped drinking, but I cannot stop the weed. I need help."

A few years later our daughter admitted that she had been binge drinking in high school and as a college freshman to the point that "I don't want to do this anymore. I need help."

Then one day our other son asked to meet, and when he came through the front door in tears he blurted, "When I drink, I drink to blackout. I need help too."

As any parent would in each of those moments when their child is suffering, I was shocked. One after another, my children admitted their problem. Everything we did to shield them from substances hadn't worked. I was scared for them. I also felt a sharp pang of shame.

But I will never forget my flush of relief and the eagerness to grab hold and hug them tight in those next few moments after they admitted their vulnerability. Or the look on their anguished faces when I assured them, "You're not in trouble for using. I am here to help you. Right now."

I was able to steer each of my children to the professional resources they needed. It wasn't easy, and there were a few missteps along their way—for them and for me. But remarkably, all three forged a way forward to wellness of mind, body, and spirit. Not along the familiar path that matches how I recover from my addiction. Though their recovery looks different than mine, there is no doubt that all three of my adult children are recovering from the desperate condition that led them to ask for help many years ago. So comfortable are they in this reality that they gave me permission to share their journeys in my public advocacy at Hazelden Betty Ford and in this book.

I am proud of them. I am proud of my role as their father too. They all reminded me, again, in their own way, that it is okay to ask for help.*

In listening to others' stories, our eyes can be opened to what is possible. Stories are powerful. They share perspectives and experiences. When we hear a story that resonates, it can move us and shake us awake. At their most fundamental level, stories connect us to each other and let us know it's okay to ask for help.

In the context of family members with loved ones struggling with

* William Cope Moyers, bestselling author and vice president of public affairs and community relations at the Hazelden Betty Ford Foundation.

addiction or in sustained recovery, listening to stories not only opens a shared connection and kindred community, it can also change the way our minds connect with the experiences of others. In this place of shared storytelling is a synchronous dance where we find meaning and we can find hope.

With eyes of compassion, we see our loved ones (regardless of where they are in their substance use journey) as human. Beautiful, despite their flaws. Deserving of love and care *just because*.

Imagine if we only received love when we deserved love.

When we share our stories vulnerably with each other, we communicate that we can return home at any time. We can have radical trust that no matter what we've been through or done or thought or left undone, there is a home waiting for us, and that home is each other.

We are deserving of love whether we are healthy in recovery, have had a slip, or are still seeking a different way to live. I share William's story and others in this book to give you hope and help you understand what choosing recovery can look like. Now, let's dive into what addiction is so you can better understand what your loved one is going through.

Remember

Recovery is a process and it's about change. It's more than sobriety or abstaining from problematic substance use; it is about improving health and wellness and living a new story.

Reflect

- How do you define addiction recovery?
- What stories do you share about your loved one?
- Is this story changing over time?

Chapter 2

Neuroscience for Normies

We are not bad people becoming good
but sick people becoming well.
—Ryan Hampton, *American Fix*

When I was seventeen and in inpatient addiction treatment for the second time after a near-fatal overdose, one of the few things I remember from my short-lived stay was a grainy video we watched on what cocaine does to the brain.

My DOC (or "drug of choice" as they say in treatment) left me depressed and hopeless. My mind ached, and I lost all joy in things that used to light me up. An almost constant state of withdrawal left me reeling from what felt like the worst flu bug. It was a desperate cycle of physical and emotional pain, longing, seeking, using, repeating. It was a ride I desperately wanted to exit, but I didn't know how to make a break.

When I saw this video though, I remember a couple light-bulb moments. Maybe what I was feeling (physical sickness, despair, anxiety, depression, not wanting to go on) was due, in part, to the side effects of heavy cocaine use and then withdrawal.

Maybe there was a reason I ended up in treatment, and it wasn't because I was bad. Maybe what was happening to me was normal when addiction takes hold of a human.

Over time I learned that cocaine and other drugs create feel-good neurotransmitters in our bodies (e.g., dopamine) at wildly high levels, and so we stop naturally producing them. In other words, there is a *reason* we feel so low in active addiction.

Drug use becomes a way not to "get high," but to maintain equilibrium. It is a way to stave off the sickness and depression. Using helps us to feel okay—even if for only a short while.

You may have heard a loved one say something like, "I have to use to feel normal." This isn't a lie. This can be true for those of us who have struggled with addiction or heavy substance use.

Now, let's unpack how neuroscience can help us learn about this process and understand more about our loved one too. It is important for us to come to terms with what addiction is before we turn our attention to what recovery is.

Are you ready?

Mind Over Gray Matter

Neuroscience points to several factors why addiction can take hold or "hijack" the brain, morphing our loved ones or ourselves into people we barely recognize. However, many researchers note that the science of addiction—and certainly recovery—is ongoing and in process. We are learning more every day. Let's not forget that centuries ago, philosophers like Aristotle thought the brain's only function was to keep the heart from overheating.[1] Sort of like coolant in a car engine. What we know today is that the brain, while lacking in the looks department, is the most advanced and complex of organs.[2]

The National Institute on Drug Abuse shares,

> This three-pound mass of gray and white matter sits at the center of all human activity—you need it to drive a car, to enjoy a meal, to breathe, to create an artistic masterpiece, and to enjoy everyday

activities. The brain regulates your body's basic functions, enables you to interpret and respond to everything you experience, and shapes your behavior. In short, *your brain is you*—everything you think and feel, and who you are.[3]

Hold up.

Let's think again about that last part: "Your brain is you."

More recent science says that the opposite is true. Dr. W. Lee Warren, author of *The Life-Changing Art of Self-Brain Surgery*, shares that "what we're really learning now is that the root of neuroplasticity is the brain's response to the mind, and that mind and brain are *not* the same thing. This is where the hope lies, because our thoughts are what drive positive brain changes, overcome addictions, and allow us to believe and know that we are not just our brains."[4]

In other words, our brains are *not* us.

And this is a hopeful thought.

As a reminder, I'm not a neuroscientist and you probably aren't either. What I can show you is a simplified way to think about how the brain works, and then how substance use and addiction can impact it.

We are not getting an advanced degree today, but we will look at a simplified version of the science so you can understand your loved one (or perhaps even your own control center) better. I also want to remind us that addiction is not only biological. There are also social, emotional, and even spiritual components to it (more on that later).

First, let's talk about the brain more generally, and then we'll move on to what happens when addiction hits.

How the Brain Works (a lesson in neuroscience for normies)

- The brain uses neurons, which are organized into circuits and neural pathway networks.
- Each neuron functions like a light switch, controlling the flow of information like sensations.

- After receiving a number of signals, the neurons send signals to one another (think texting back and forth after the latest Netflix series hits); these signals travel through the body via the nervous system.
- All the interconnected parts of the brain work together, with different circuits and neurons responsible for different functions.
- To send messages and signals (using the texting example), neurons write the text (neurotransmitter) and then send it via the Wi-Fi connection (synapse) to a bestie (another neuron).
- Neurons (people getting the text) receive it, read, and react (emoji). Reactions could mean passing the message along to someone else.
- The transporter molecule (or the "someone else" reading the text) receives the message, and then the message circles back to the original sender.

But what happens when substances like drugs or alcohol enter the picture or substance use develops into addiction? How can this impact normal brain functioning—and why does this matter? How do the messages get interrupted or intercepted?

This Is (Really) Your Brain on Drugs

A healthy brain has a good balance of neurotransmitters keeping your mood steady and your body functioning the way it's supposed to. But when you introduce addiction, things go haywire. Ever been on a road trip and you lose cell reception? It's sort of like that. Frantic disconnection.

With initial use of a substance, the brain gets a flood of feel-good chemicals like dopamine, creating a sense of euphoria or a "high." I'm not going to lie. At first, this might feel pretty good. It can be exciting. And more than that, for those of us who begin using drugs or alcohol to relieve some type of emotional pain or trauma, it can quickly become a welcome solution.

But over time, with ongoing use, the brain's reward system becomes overstimulated, releasing too much dopamine. Because our bodies are incredibly designed, our brains try to find a balance again and stop producing feel-good chemicals naturally. The excitement soon wears off, and tolerance develops.

When addiction or substance use disorder begins, the brain tries to cope by cutting back its natural dopamine production and lowering sensitivity to it. This is when you begin to need more of the substance to feel normal. We seek that euphoric feeling, but it is always just out of reach: a maddening cycle that we can't escape.

When the substance is taken away, withdrawal sets in and the brain is left with too little dopamine and other key neurotransmitters.

This is how I entered treatment as a teen and how I then experienced too many harrowing days with withdrawal symptoms like shaking, sweating, nausea, depression, and intense cravings. Depending on the substance, some withdrawal symptoms can even be fatal (like with alcohol or benzodiazepines).

Over time, repeated use of substances can change the structure of the brain—especially the prefrontal cortex, which helps with decision-making and self-control. This can lead to memory loss, poor judgment, and emotional instability.

Ultimately, "the brain's response to a drug is always to facilitate the opposite state; therefore, the only way for any regular user to feel normal is to take the drug. Getting high, if it occurs at all, is increasingly short-lived, and so the purpose of using is to stave off withdrawal."[5]

Doesn't sound very fun, does it?

For those of us who struggle with addiction, chasing the first high is a destination that is never found. No matter how hard we try, tolerance (along with other factors) will never let us get to that "first high feeling." Substance use changes from being a choice to choosing us.

Tolerance can be deadly, too, with many overdose fatalities occurring after people stop using substances for a time (like during incarceration). When people have a period of abstinence and then go back to using the same amount, they discover that their body is not ready for that amount again (even though their mind might be).

Tragically, we have lost many loved ones because of this.*

Importantly, understanding the neuroscience of addiction can help us to understand our loved ones in new ways:

- When they experience depression or extreme sadness or loss of interest in things they used to love.
- When they are physically destroyed or sick.
- When addiction appears to change the one we love into someone we don't recognize.

When this happens, we can reflect back on what is happening at a neurochemical level.

The good news is that neuroscience can also help us understand the healing and renewal that can happen with the recovery process. Like we now know the brain is much more than an organ to cool off our overheating hearts, we know our brains can heal in recovery.

This Is Your Brain on Recovery

We know that substance use and addiction negatively impact the brain, but how does recovery help heal the control center of the mind,

* If you have lost a loved one to addiction or overdose fatality, my heart goes out to you. No one should ever have to experience that pain. I'm so glad you are reading this book and encourage you to spend time with the section in the back titled, "A Note on Grief."

body, and emotions? Everyone from neuroscientists to theologians has theories on how or why the brain heals.

Andrew Newberg, who wrote *How God Changes Your Brain*, shares that we can play an active role in the brain-healing process. By "actively participating in our own neural construction" we can partner in the neuroplasticity that many believe God created our minds with. When we shift our attention from substance use to recovery, or as in the case of Newberg's theory from the world to God, our brains and minds can be renewed.[6]

Theologian and brain surgeon (yes, I said that) Dr. W. Lee Warren shares that

> your brain is constantly making new synapses, breaking old ones, and wiring neurons together in a way that makes brain habits get stronger with repetition and die off with disuse (neuroplasticity, or the brain's ability to change when directed to by mind-down control). Hebb's Law is the famous, "Neurons that fire together, wire together," so let's make that work for us instead of against us.
>
> You can harness the power of neuroplasticity to unlearn harmful patterns, reinforce helpful ones, break free from destructive old stories and limiting beliefs, and overcome anything that is holding you back.[7]

In other words, the brain can heal.

We are not permanently damaged. The brain is resilient and powerful. People in recovery can go on to live healthy, purposeful, and joyful lives.[8] All with healed brains and bodies.

• • • • •

When we love someone in recovery, remember that our actions—healthy actions—can rewire our brain.

• • • • •

The Recovery Research Institute shares a growing body of evidence that addiction recovery can heal the brain long-term.[9]

One study on adolescent alcohol use disorder recovery shows that brain imaging scans taken over time reveal a return of normal functioning in the part of the brain impacted by alcohol, the prefrontal cortex.[10] Other studies indicate that the longer the abstinence from substances, the higher the increase in improvements to executive functioning.[11]

Here are other ways the brain can heal through recovery:

- **Restoration of balance:** Recovery can restore the brain's system of balance through the release of neurotransmitters such as dopamine and serotonin, which lead to feeling "normal" and even good without the use of substances.
- **Improvement of cognitive functioning:** Memory, attention, and even problem-solving can all improve as the brain returns to equilibrium during recovery.
- **Reduction of stress:** Recovery can lead to a more balanced state of neurotransmitters and, in turn, reduce anxiety.
- **Function and structure of the brain:** As mentioned above, studies suggest that areas like the prefrontal cortex, which are impacted by substance use, can return to a more normal state and function regularly again.

Judy Grisel shares this: "It is beginning to seem that the brain is more like a stage for our life to be acted out upon than like the director behind a curtain calling shots."[12] Our brain's primary functions are to respond and to adapt to the world around us. To send and receive signals. When we do all of this *in recovery*, our brains function in a healthier and more balanced way. Our lives can be in harmony with our whole selves again.

Recovery and Relapse

It is important to note that sometimes relapse or recurrence of use is a part of the process of recovery, like a medical condition in remission can have a resurgence (cancer, heart disease, or diabetes). That does not mean we are any less welcome to be embraced by loved ones or the recovery community with open, trusting arms.

It may take a while for us to damage our minds and brains through substance use and addiction. Healing takes time too.

A relapse or recurrence of use does not have to be the cause of a closed door to a relationship. It can be a sign that we are human and we still need help and support.

Hopefully this science lesson helped you understand a bit more fully, and perhaps compassionately, about your loved one's addiction and the hope that your brain—in all of its neuroplasticity, gray matter, and wonder—can heal. We can begin to understand our loved ones in a new way and perhaps begin to trust that a new story is possible.

And yet . . .

You may be coming from a place of immense hurt, distrust, or shame. Believing anything new about the *why* of your loved one's struggles, like neuroscience, may be tough. You may be tired. You may be afraid that "this time it's going to be different" and "recovery is going to work" won't be true. I get that. I've been there with my own loved ones.

You may also have a tough time hearing that addiction isn't a choice. Especially after having experienced deep pain or hurt. Doesn't this idea remove personal responsibility or accountability for our loved one's choices?

As we journey along together, I'd like to ask you to stay with me. We are going to continue exploring these topics. You love someone in recovery—or seeking recovery—because you are still reading. Let's keep going.

Remember

Understanding addiction neuroscience can help reduce addiction recovery stigma for both people in recovery and their family members.

Reflect

Explain in your own words the science of addiction. How does this give you hope that your loved one can heal—body, mind, and spirit?

Chapter 3

The Recovery Journey

Rethinking anything is hard.
—Christina Dent, *Curious: A Foster Mom's Discovery of an Unexpected Solution to Drugs and Addiction*

I'm going to be real with you for a minute. The first time I heard about the concept of harm reduction, I shook my head like any good 12-stepper.

A recovery pathway other than those found *in the rooms*?

Sharing visibly and vocally about recovery outside of church basements?

Beginning a recovery journey by taking actions that reduce harm but don't necessarily begin with abstinence?

I've had well-intentioned and loving people tell me that the only way to get sober is to do the 12 steps of Alcoholics Anonymous. Other people—again, with good intentions—shared that the only way was to attend Celebrate Recovery and do the workbooks religiously. Others insisted that you must commit to SMART Recovery or Life Recovery or Re:generation Recovery or that you must stay away from medications for addiction treatment like medications for opioid use disorder (MOUD) or—fill in the blank. We human beings like to create lines to live within and outside of. We like our rules because, let's face it, sometimes rules keep us safe.

For many people (I'm raising my hand here), there are recovery pathways that save our lives and save our souls in many ways. We are going to explore some of the many ways people can find their way *to* recovery and continue on the path.

The longer I've been in recovery, the more difficulty I've had with these ultimatums (or perhaps this is my comfort with breaking the rules). Either way, here are important things for family members and loved ones to know:

- Just because your loved one goes to AA or NA or any of the *A*'s does not mean they will maintain sobriety or recovery.
- Just because they go to a faith-based program does not mean they will have a newfound or renewed love of the church and Jesus *and* stay in recovery.
- Just because your loved one practices harm reduction, using safe injection sites or smoking cannabis instead of crack, does not mean that they will be healthy, healed, and whole.

I say all of this not to discourage you but to encourage you: If one way isn't working for your loved one, it doesn't mean that is the end of the road. Sometimes one approach is a stepping stone to another. Check out the appendix where I dig deeper into various pathways. Research shows that many factors play a role in someone finding and maintaining recovery.* This is part of why I'm sharing this book with you: to unpack what recovery means, what it means when we love someone in recovery, and what we must understand to support them. One of the most important ways to do this is by listening and learning.

A couple of years ago my church invited me to share about my second book, *You Are Not Your Trauma*, in a three-week book study

---

* I'd like to make sure that the distinction is clear: When I say there are many pathways to recovery, this does not equate to many pathways to salvation. Some communities feel that the "many pathways" concept refers to other areas (like faith). In this context I'm speaking solely about addiction recovery. Read on to keep exploring this together.

with a group of church members who had been meeting regularly on Sunday mornings before services, some for nearly fifty years. This was a group of people that were well-dressed and well-versed in their Christian faith. Pleated khakis and fresh permed curls abounded. What I wasn't prepared for were the poignant yet simple questions they asked that made me rethink everything I thought I knew about recovery.

One woman turned to me and asked, "What is recovery?"

Of course, I sort of chuckled to myself because she didn't know me well and didn't know that my entire life, both personally and professionally, had been fused with the concept. No person (aside from my then five-year-old son) had ever flat-out asked me this question.

The woman continued: "My sister is an alcoholic and has struggled for years. She says she's in recovery, but I don't understand it. She's been in and out of treatment. Goes to meetings, I think. But what is it? What does it mean?"

What I shared with this church member is that recovery can be an individualized path. There isn't a cookie-cutter approach. Just like everyone's treatment and recovery from other human conditions and struggles may be different from that of their neighbor who is going through the same thing. I also shared that there are different approaches to recovery, an entire menu of options, similar to how someone undergoing cancer treatment has options like chemotherapy, radiation, medications, or even surgery.

Recovery is not linear, going from point A (addiction) to point R (recovery) in a straight line. There are detours, twists, and turns, as in all of life.

I wish I could paint a picture of what the woman's eyes looked like when I turned back toward her after sharing these pieces and more (that we will cover in later chapters).

"Thank you," she said with a sense of calm and assurance. "I understand more now."

The History of Recovery

While I connect with this broader view of recovery, the concept itself has evolved with an interesting history. According to researchers, in 1939 there was a cultural shift beginning after a publication from Alcoholics Anonymous titled "How more than one hundred men have recovered from alcoholism."[1] The experience of AA and its growing success at that time led individuals and families to start shifting from merely a focus on "stopping drinking" to one of recovery maintenance.

Fast-forward a couple of decades and by 1982, the American Society of Addiction Medicine entered the picture and began to note that recovery was "a state of physical and psychological health."[2] While an emphasis on abstinence-based recovery was still the norm, this was the beginning of viewing recovery in a broader sense, one that incorporated a whole-health approach to wellness instead of a one-size-fits-all model.

Rewind and you will see that humanity has been dealing with addiction recovery for a long time. Even Jesus turned water into wine and the people likely cheered (the ones with a questionable relationship to said wine, perhaps a bit more loudly).

Here is a brief history. Note that this timeline is admittedly limited, with countless groups from various cultures and countries not included. This would have to be its own book if I were to include everything that is known or recorded.*

- **3400 BCE, Mesopotamia:** Sumerians cultivate opium poppies, referring to them as the "joy plant."
- **Ancient Egypt:** Hieroglyphics reference alcohol misuse.

---

* William White's *Slaying the Dragon: The History of Addiction Treatment and Recovery in America* (Chestnut Health Systems, 1998) offers an incredible picture of the history of addiction and recovery in the United States.

- **Greeks and Romans:** Philosophical discussions occur about intoxication and excess, with gods like Dionysus symbolizing the mix of "divine inspiration" and dangerous excess.
- **Philosophers Plato and Aristotle:** Warned against excessive drinking and pondered the nature of habit and virtue.
- **Medieval church influence:** Substance use was viewed as a sin.
- **Twelfth century:** Invention of distillation increases alcohol potency and availability, thus increasing rates of substance-use issues.
- **Renaissance medical theories:** A recognition of physical and psychological factors that contribute to addiction emerges. Paracelsus introduces the use of opium in medical practice.
- **Industrialization/urbanization:** Overcrowding, poor working conditions, and social alienation contribute to a new culture of substance use for coping with stress and the hardship of daily life.
- **Nineteenth century:** Rise of patented medicines containing opiates and cocaine, which were prescribed over the counter for anything from headaches to "woman troubles." Early organized attempts at addiction treatment began, including the New York State Inebriate Asylum in 1864.
- **Early addiction treatment centers:** 1879 saw the establishment of the Keeley Institute along with the emergence of scientific cures for alcoholism.
- **Twentieth century:** The temperance movement starts, which focuses on curbing alcohol consumption and leads to Prohibition in the 1920s.
- **Alcoholics Anonymous (1935):** The introduction of peer support and a new 12-step program with Christian roots influences future addiction-treatment approaches.

- **1980s–2000s:** Research advances and brain imaging technologies shed light on addiction as a chronic brain disease.
- **Holistic treatment approaches (2000s on):** An emphasis on psychological and social factors of addiction recovery emerges, including the development of evidence-based practices like cognitive behavioral therapy and motivational interviewing for addiction treatment.
- **Personalized treatment plans:** A consideration of genetics, personal history, trauma and adverse childhood experiences, and co-occurring mental health conditions expands into the field.
- **Pharmacological treatments:** Medications like naltrexone and buprenorphine offer new hope for opioid use disorder.

Like the evolution of substance use, recovery is a process. It is not a straight line from struggle to healing but a movement of understanding. It is all nestled inside a complex historical context (limited in many ways) that combines evolving scientific knowledge, substance use trends and perceptions, and other factors. It is not surprising, then, that to get there or maintain recovery (a continual *getting there*) can be a multifaceted approach. One of the most helpful insights along this journey is through a concept called *recovery capital*.

Recovery Capital Changes the Game

Recovery capital is a concept introduced by researchers William Cloud and Robert Granfield in a book called *Coming Clean: Overcoming Addiction Without Treatment*.[3] They describe it as the resources, assets, and protective factors that help an individual begin a recovery pathway or pathways and sustain the journey long-term.

This concept instantly revolutionized the way people understood, practiced, and supported recovery.

Wait.

Actually, no, it didn't. Not immediately. Unfortunately, it took twenty years before the concept started gaining traction outside of academic circles. It also took the efforts, advocacy, and research of an affected family member, Dr. David Best.

> The origins of recovery capital come from the concept of "social capital" which refers to the idea that, even for people with no money (traditional financial capital) there are other valuable resources that people can have that link to the networks and supports they can access both in times of need and in their everyday lives. Someone to pick you up from the airport, to help you decorate the spare bedroom or even someone who can tell you what is important and new in your neighbourhood.* These are all valuable resources although they have no monetary value.[4]

The "breadth and depth of internal and external resources available to support someone in their recovery journey," according to Best, are key to unlocking something new about the way that we support our loved ones.[5] The main predictor of long-term success in abstinence-based recovery is not the absence of something or removing or stopping a substance.[6] It is about introducing new things. It is about adding strengths.

Dr. Best echoes this sentiment and is spending his academic career traveling the world and talking to communities about recovery capital, along with how a model of growth and strength can be especially important for family members. As a researcher, Best shares, "What inspired my interest in the idea was that here was something that could be counted and measured potentially overcoming the

---

* If you don't have friends in the United Kingdom, you may think that I misspelled the word *neighborhood* in the quote. My friends and colleagues in the UK, like Dr. Best, have all sorts of funny spellings for things (don't get me started on the word *organisation*), along with wit and charm.

criticism that recovery is a vague, nebulous, and ultimately unscientific concept."[7]

Recovery capital is key for family members and will help illuminate our collective understanding of how someone can recover, regardless of the pathway or pathways they might start or end on. It is about strength, assets, and resources. It is about the protective factors we build up against the hardships that inevitably come in life, whether we struggle with addiction or not.

Recovery capital broadens the conversation about what helps our loved ones get better and it helps us to understand treatment in a new way. Keeping this in mind helps us consider that there are many things that can support our loved one.

Treatment, for example, can mean more than a ten-day inpatient stay (as it did for me back in 2000). Inpatient or outpatient treatment is often a key step along the path, but so are things like social support from peers and meaningful work and volunteer opportunities and communities to connect with and renewed purpose through parenting classes or outdoor activity groups or . . . the list of types of recovery capital goes on and on.

• • • • •

When you love someone in recovery, understand that recovery is about more than treatment for the *use* of substances. It is about *change* and enhancing a quality of life that makes us want to stay *in recovery* with purpose.

• • • • •

Christi Hildebran, vice president of research and evaluation at Comagine Health, a nonprofit health-care consulting firm, breaks down the concept in additional ways from outside of academia.[8] She calls recovery capital the "building blocks of recovery." For our loved ones, recovery capital provides support and stability, increases coping mechanisms, and enhances resilience and a sense of agency or empowerment. These are all central to a long-term, sustained recovery.

Let's take a closer look at the different types. The Substance Abuse and Mental Health Services Administration (SAMHSA) defines recovery capital in four primary, tangible areas:

1. **Physical:** This includes elements that lead to safe and stable living environments and meeting of basic needs. Housing, transportation, employment, health care access, food, and clothing are all examples of physical capital and essential for building a healthy recovery. Unfortunately, many individuals, especially in rural areas, struggle with aspects of physical capital like transportation. This can create a domino effect, leading to less access to other recovery capital that is essential for support (and sometimes even survival).
2. **Human:** This is an internal type of capital that often needs to be encouraged over time. For many of us, human capital centers on the concept of identity. Many of us lose this or never find or feel a secure sense of self. Building things like personal health and wellness and education, along with internal attributes like resilience, hope, confidence, and coping skills, are key to this type of capital. Having a sense of agency in our own lives and stronger mental health can help us persevere when recovery gets challenging (which it invariably will, as in life) and lead to a sense of calm and confidence in the storm.
3. **Social:** This includes the social interactions and relationships from family (biological or chosen), friends, recovery community members, and others. Safe and trusting relationships can provide important protective factors, role models, and accountability that lead to learning other humans *can* be trusted and safe. For many of us, extreme isolation (often self-inflicted), along with trauma, can lead us to unhealthy

reliance on self or isolating from healthy support. Over time, learning how to rely on and trust social connection is key to this type of recovery capital and ultimately, a healthy recovery for the long run.

4. **Cultural:** This centers on specific beliefs or attitudes, even values, that connect to one's identity and community. It can also be derived from familial ties or other characteristics of identity. For example, my personal faith informs my cultural recovery capital. For others it could be resources that include culturally sensitive services such as language accessibility or peer support provision by a provider with a similar background or ethnicity or set of experiences.

Recovery includes each of these areas. We need security and safety through the meeting of our basic human needs (physical recovery capital). We thrive with a new, healthy sense of identity and the qualities, like resilience, that can help us sustain wholeness (human recovery capital). We become a part of community and find our foundation when we learn that we belong (social recovery capital). We become a part of a bigger story and discover deep personal faith or connection within our chosen families (cultural recovery capital).

Researchers and advocates alike continue to build off this broadened view of recovery by including those things which strengthen our outer and inner lives.

Recovery is a continuum. It isn't one-size-fits-all. It includes everything from prevention programs and education to harm reduction methods to long-term assistance like recovery housing or employment support. Each option offers something different for different stages of the journey.

When I connect with people in recovery at events I am speaking at or in our local community, I am always struck by the fact that people in recovery are resilient. Most of us aren't born with a set of strong coping skills or know intuitively how to handle stress or other hardships life sends our way. Through the journey and through the recovery pathways that help us get here, we learn how to be healthy.* We grow internally as our external supports get stronger. The pieces of the recovery capital puzzle fit together to help us build our lives anew.

• • • • •

When you love someone in recovery, it's important to keep in mind that recovery is about increased quality of life, not just sobriety.

• • • • •

Recovery and, importantly, sustained recovery, is about so much more than "going to treatment" or "getting sober."

In the back of the book, I have included more information and examples of different recovery pathways. I've also included a helpful matrix adapted from the original recovery capital measure, which can help as a guide for loved ones—a North Star of where to focus attention as they are on their own path or pathways of recovery. As we've shared together, recovery is not only "going to treatment," although treatment can be a great starting point and provide much-needed ongoing support. There is also a bigger picture, a more expansive way to look at it—and families and other loved ones can play an integral role in discovering what's next.

* Check out "Recovery Pathways" at the back of this book to learn more.

Remember

There are multiple pathways of recovery. Loved ones may practice different pathways during different phases of their recovery process.

Reflect

- What recovery pathway(s) is your loved one on?
- How can you commit to learning more about these pathways and supporting your loved one on their journey to building resilience?

PART 2

recovery is hope

Chapter 4

Supporting Does Not Mean Enabling

Stop breaking your heart. Learn to
love people for who they are and not
how you imagined them to be.
—Kierra C. T. Banks

My dad picked me up from the run-down apartment where I was living temporarily with a couple of girls who had recently graduated high school. Cans of Mountain Dew with ash sprinkled on the top, floating cigarette butts, crusty dishes piled high by the sink, probably rats or cockroaches or both waltzing across the old wooden floors, but I didn't notice. I was too high. Too sad. Too desperate.

When I stepped out into the daylight—something unusual for my then routine of keeping vampire hours—my dad took one look at me and started to tear up.

"Oh, honey."

He shook his head and pulled me into him and wrapped his arms around me. I felt like I was four years old again, slow dancing across bronze ceramic kitchen tiles, my little feet on his feet. I breathed in and smelled Old Spice and peppermint. I felt his whiskers on my forehead as I nuzzled in and started to weep.

"I'm tired, Dad."

After a long embrace, something that I needed, he took me grocery shopping: something else that I desperately needed. When I had an appetite, which wasn't often, I lived off Lipton noodles and soda and whatever scraps were left over from my friends' dinner.

Then he took me to Country Kitchen, and I pushed an omelet around with my fork. He asked me about the future, and I told him I wanted to go to college and I wanted to write books. I started to see in his eyes a glimmer of possibility for me.

Maybe there was hope for me yet.

Maybe I could grow up to be someone.

Maybe yet, I could dream.

You see, I didn't know it at the time, but the simple actions of showing up and providing tangible support, even just an embrace, was what I needed. I didn't need tough love. I didn't need my family to turn their backs on me. I didn't need to be left alone.

I needed someone to have hope for me.

I needed love, community, and recovery.

Just like I'd never before experienced being in active addiction and the stress, unease, and distress of a roaring substance use disorder, they'd never raised a teenager whose brain, body, emotions, and spirit were crushed. They didn't know about my being sexually assaulted, bullied, or any of the other challenges I was facing as a teen. They didn't know my acting out and dishonesty and hiding was my immature attempt at trying to control an out-of-control life. Quiet my trauma. Tame my addiction.

Now that I've been in recovery for fifteen years and counting and have worked in helping fields for over two decades, I've encountered thousands of family members who are in or were in the same situation as my parents back then, their eyes bloodshot and pleading.

How do I support them?

What do I support them toward?

Should I stay present with them in this and risk enabling their behavior, or should I turn away?

Did I cause their addiction?

How did I not notice sooner?

Can they ever recover?

How can I help them?

Will I ever find peace to live my own life?

What could I have done to prevent this?

What can I do to fix it?

I've also been on the other side as a family member and affected loved one myself. Asking these mountains of questions. Pleading. Searching for answers.

Perhaps, like me, you've heard advice from well-meaning friends, family, or even therapists or addiction treatment providers:

They need to hit rock bottom before they can accept help.

Helping them is codependent.

You are enabling them.

You must cut all ties.

There is nothing you can do.[1]

Maybe you have felt the deep pain, frustration, confusion, and desperation from where these statements can lead.

We want to be able to support our loved ones. We want to believe that we don't have to shut them out to love them or encourage them to walk through the doors of recovery.

For family members whose loved ones are in recovery and sustaining it, we also want to believe that it is real this time. That recovery works. That lasting change is possible.

Tough Love or Something Else?

Love is tough. Ask any family who has supported their loved one through addiction into recovery or who has lost a loved one to substance use. You may know this truth more deeply than some.

Your loved one got out of treatment—again—and you don't know if you believe it's going to work—*again*.

Your spouse admitted that they have a problem with alcohol and you aren't sure how to support them or what to do next.

You started dating someone in recovery and have no idea what this means or what it means for your relationship.

Your best friend celebrated one year in recovery and you'd love to be able to celebrate too.

Love is tough, yet it is also patient. Hopeful. Forgiving. Understanding.

But how do we choose love when we have been hurt so deeply by our loved one? How do we trust that recovery is real *this time*? How can we show up in loving and informed ways to support those we care about who are committed to a recovery journey? How can we have hope even if evidence to the contrary surrounds us?

I'm not sure how you are showing up today as you read these words, but I have a feeling that I know at least part of why you picked up this book. It's the reason I've felt compelled—called, even—to write it. Maybe you feel a sense of both "I'm over it" (your loved one's addiction or recovery) and a desire to show up and support them. I get it and have been there. I've felt equally frustrated and afraid of my loved one's use or recovery.

There are millions of us, of affected family members and loved ones, who want to understand addiction recovery and how to show up for and support our loved ones. "What we believe and think about matters," and I am here to challenge us to reframe.[2]

We can move toward a new (and evidence-based) approach to supporting our loved ones. We can rewrite our family's story to include more hope and less frantic worry, despair, and darkness. We can learn what it means to be in addiction recovery and grow together toward a healthier way to cope.

I trust in other experts, the research, and what God has to say about that matter. Even if you don't agree with that last part, maybe today you can suspend your uncertainty, table your doubt, and take a risk. Try listening without judgment and with curiosity.

I love the hopeful call from other researchers on family recovery who say, "If your own optimism has gotten shaky in recent months or years, we invite you to borrow ours for now. Take this book like a steadying hand. And know that you can make a difference."[3]

Let's Reframe the Story

Back in the late 1990s when I was struggling with addiction, I didn't know there was something called *recovery* that I needed to access to save my life. My parents didn't know either.

Today things are different. There are countless recovery options, like a menu at an Asian fusion restaurant—even if (sadly) not everyone has the same access to these supports (like women of color, those who are pregnant or parenting, and other under-resourced people, to name a few). Studies estimate that there are over twenty million of us (people in recovery) in the United States alone.[4]

Today we don't have the luxury of ignorance. At the tips of our fingers are countless resources, meetings, and directions.

And our loved ones, regardless of what their outward behavior is telling us, depend on us to be able to show up. When we struggle with our own challenges, we need family and community to step up and be there to support us. It doesn't matter what our thing is—substance use or something else (food, phone, porn, grief, shopping, gambling)—that keeps us stuck and in patterns of behavior that create consequences that don't line up with our hopes for our lives or our values. We all need support and encouragement. We all need to be understood and loved. Not because we are perfect, but in our humanness.

But I also acknowledge that it is tough, especially after considering my own family's experience and talking with countless parents and loved ones who have walked the excruciating road of addiction. It's tough to know how to show up in a way that truly helps another person.

In a recent article, I learned about a Massachusetts family who was trying to support their son Brendan with an opioid use disorder. This family was told to show tough love to their son by a treatment center: "They went to peer support groups [the family]. And while helpful, Ken (Brendan's dad) says the advice was clear. Distance yourself from your loved one or you're enabling, almost like putting a syringe in your child's arm."

What they learned over time, however, was that it was the opposite that would help their son the most. They learned how to love him with healthy boundaries. Just like my dad showed up for me years ago.

My dad didn't give me a wad of cash *and* he didn't stop answering the phone. He saw a need (I was hungry), and he did what he could.

Alicia Ventura from Boston Medical Center says that due to the deadly crisis posed by newer drugs like fentanyl, family recovery interventions need to evolve: "We need to start trying new things. And part of that, really, is going to be improving their interactions with their families and taking advantage of these people who innately love them and want to care for them."[5]

Have you experienced similar advice to what Brendan's family did? Cut all ties or you are enabling and causing harm? Has your family wondered how tough love is helping—if it is helping—or have your insides been twisted in knots over how you've been encouraged to support?

Perhaps, as Alicia Ventura shares, we need to think differently about how to support our loved ones. Perhaps it can be not about turning away but about how to communicate and who to bring into a circle of support. Perhaps we've all given too much power to the idea that support of any kind is reinforcing problematic substance use. There is a difference between loving and enabling.

Is Enabling a Myth?

In some recovery spaces *enabling* is like the plague. If your loved one is struggling with addiction, you must avoid it at all costs. This is a death sentence, and if you do it, if you *enable* them, your loved one will never stop using again. You must step away, wait for them to hit "rock bottom," and then pray. If they aren't getting better, well, maybe you aren't praying hard enough.

This, of course, is more than a bit tongue in cheek.

Part of why I've written this book is to challenge our ways of seeing and doing things as they relate to our loved one's recovery journey. This may, for you, include looking at the ways we think about some of these concepts like the tough love approach or the concept of enabling.

Can we care for our loved ones in a way that is unhealthy (for them or for us)? Yes, absolutely.

Do we need help discerning how to set healthy boundaries? Of course.

Do some of us need to learn how to have "strategic detachment" when our loved ones may be under the influence? Certainly.

But according to Merriam-Webster, enabling means "to provide with the means or opportunity . . . to make possible, practical, or easy."[6]

There is a difference between enabling and reinforcing. Reinforcement works to provide positive feedback and praise for action. This creates cyclical action. The more positive actions and change our loved one makes—the longer we walk a recovery road—the more positive feedback. Thus, the cycle continues. As family members and loved ones, we can reinforce ideas and behaviors (more on this in a bit), but we cannot enable or directly cause them.

Let me say this again:

As family members and loved ones, we can reinforce ideas and behaviors, but we cannot enable or directly cause them.

Nothing you can do will enable your loved one to keep using substances—they will do this all by themselves. Trust me, I've done the research. My friends have too. It is our choice to use that fifty-dollar bill for our next hit and not a parking ticket, gas, or groceries.

What we can do as family members is commit to understanding the recovery process. We can commit to leaning into what the research and our personal experiences tell us about what works in terms of support. We can also extend love and grace in evidence-based ways that *encourage* our loved ones and help us stay sane (with boundaries) in the process. We are going to get into the specifics of how to do this in later chapters of this book, too, so please keep reading.

In her book *Addict in the Family: Stories of Loss, Hope, and Recovery*, Beverly Conyers, an author and recovery advocate whose daughter struggled with addiction, says this about her experience of walking alongside her loved one:

> Addiction would come to dominate her life and mine far into the future. I became more familiar than I ever wanted to be with things like detox, treatment, recovery, relapse, and the criminal justice system. I lived with deep anxiety and burgeoning hope

> and devastating disappointment. I learned about boundaries and detachment and letting go, about frustration and expectations and humility and forgiveness. And through it all, I learned about the boundless human capacity for starting over. And then starting over again.[7]

While Beverly went through the school of hard knocks when it came to addiction, struggling with her own teetering between "Am I enabling?" to "How can I love you more?" she also learned about the other side of the struggle. The hope. The light. The opportunities to start again. And again. As she states so beautifully, she learned about the "boundless human capacity for starting over."[8]

But how can we keep showing up for our loved one when we might be gripped by yet another heartache, lie, or struggle our loved one has put us through?

My years in active addiction were a hopeless time for me. Hopeless to the point of wondering if death was easier. *Is there really anything to live for?* I remember thinking this on repeat.

My experience as an affected family member has been equally as challenging in many ways. Waiting for change, praying for change, waiting for absent love. A familiar hopelessness.

Maybe you've seen your loved one's eyes dark and heavy. The trauma of substance use, the secret life they've lived, and the horrors of what you don't know has happened to them or that they've done like heavy stones weighing them down. As pastor and author John Eldredge shares, "Trauma sensitizes you to more trauma and brings to the surface past trauma. You don't get used to it; each new crisis simply piles on the stress."[9]

When there is no hope, there is no possibility that things will change, no motivation to work or dream toward a future. When the traumas multiply, addiction can continue to run rampant in the family, workplace, church, or relationship. This leads to more stress and more heaviness.

In my teens I remember thinking that I would not survive to see my thirtieth birthday. It was almost as if I wore this hopelessness as a badge of (dis)honor. What is there to live for if there is nothing to hope, nothing to dream? If all our desires for life are deferred with nothing to fix our eyes on? If hope is a home where we feel warmth, love, and support, then hopelessness is a cold alley. In the dark there is no way to see forward.

Yet in recovery, we find there is another way. A lighter way.

The Science of Hope

The University of Oklahoma is a sprawling campus with a medieval-looking library at its center, older buildings spotted among new construction like most older universities in the states. Among its offerings and research focus areas is one that may lead us to an interesting finding as we continue on our journey into how to understand and support our loved ones.

The Hope Research Center states that they "consider hope as a theory of change required for individuals, families, organizations, and whole communities."[10] A small team of academics, professors, and researchers look at hope-centered programs and evaluate effectiveness as well as conduct-applied research projects on this important "theory of change."

Their research finds that hope is a key factor in developing resilience and increased overall psychological well-being.[11] What's more is that hope theory identifies important facets that impact a person's ability to change that we will explore, such as goals, pathways, and agency (more on this in a minute). Hope is not a feeling; it's an action.

In recovery circles, part of the magic (or holy mystery) that happens in our lives is because of sharing of hope through storytelling. Not just the gory, gritty, and sordid (though we hear plenty of those stories too). We are surrounded by living pictures of hope.

The mother who is able to get her kids back after working with probation and parole, DCS, and more.

The brother who loses the resentment in his heart and softens to heal from the anger and neglect of his childhood.

The friend who does a complete turn and decides to pursue a life serving others after losing everything because of her alcoholism.

When we hear stories of total life change and see living pictures of hope in recovery circles (whether that is in the basement in 12-step fellowships or other recovery pathways), the power of hope is unleashed.

The Hope Research Center also shares three components of hope identified from their research: goals, pathways, and agency.[12]

1. **Goals:** These are the "endpoints" for which we and our loved one's sights may be aiming. We may have hope for their sobriety, yet a large part of attaining that (as we will come to find out later) involves purpose. Goals can act as motivators and focal points for our pursuit of sobriety. But as affected loved ones, it's key that we understand that goals are about more than stopping our substance use. Working toward employment, educational, missional, even relationship goals, can help us build a fulfilling life.
2. **Pathways:** There is a new(ish) trend in the recovery advocacy space and at the federal level in the states that talks about the concept of "multiple pathways" of recovery. I've always loved this concept because it is expansive and welcoming of all the many ways folks enter and find recovery. But I recently learned how it is connected to the science of hope. A belief in pathways of recovery and wellness offers, according to the Hope Research Center, a "mental road map allowing us to consider multiple strategies that will lead to the desired outcome." Thus there is a spacious place where someone can consider many ways to get to their desired life of recovery—or for some, perhaps many paths.

3. **Agency:** This concept emphasizes the ability of our loved ones to have choice and willpower over the things they can control. It removes the sense of despair that so many of us in active addiction experience when we feel our lives are spinning out of control and we have no ability to be active participants in the change process. As family members, understanding that our loved ones must have agency (and feel that they have agency) over their own lives is key, even if only in small ways. Especially when many of us in addiction recovery have traumatic histories (experiencing things we haven't been able to control), to learn that there are things we can control is key. We can control, for example, how we respond in conflict, where we grab that cup of coffee, or what time we wake up and if we make our beds in the morning. Sometimes the small choices add up and help us understand that we can have agency over big life choices too.

These three areas are important to consider when we think about how to understand and support our loved one. When my family supported my goals, I began believing that I could attain them. When they understood that recovery is a varied landscape with many pathways, their understanding changed about what I needed for support and what I needed to do. Finally, when my family empowered my agency in my recovery journey, something beautiful happened: Hope was born. For both them—and me.

Again, hope is not a feeling; it's an action. We can have hope, be hopeful, and share hope when we understand that to hope for our loved one is not only to desire that they stop using alcohol and other drugs. Or to pray for their healing. It is to show them (through words and deeds) that no matter what they might do or not do, whether we consider them to be in recovery or not, if they are breathing, there is a possibility for life change.

The research is clear on this point too. When we have hope for our loved ones, they are more likely to get well.[13] Encouraging goals, supporting multiple pathways or strategies, and supporting agency or choice are all evidence-based ways to build hope.

• • • • •

When you love someone in recovery, you can remember that hope is not only a feeling; it's a strategy to help support your loved one.

• • • • •

When we have hope for our loved ones, we are not only sharing what feels like a warm and loving embrace. We are contributing to the reality that hope itself can support our loved ones and act as a motivator. We can replace our focus on enabling our loved ones with hoping for them. Hoping *with* them. Sharing tangible support like a meal, a hug, a grocery run, a phone call, a bed to sleep in. Connecting them with other people who can extend that hope for us when we still aren't ready to love in the way that we'd like. When the burn of pain is a bit too close and trust is still being rebuilt.

A friend of mine commented on one of my *Circle of Chairs* Substack letters: "Knowing we're loved is perhaps as close to heaven as we will ever get, but when it comes down to it, if that's all there is, maybe that's enough. A mother's love, for me, is enough to keep that hope alive."[14]

When we hope, we tell our loved ones we believe in them.

When we hope, we say that recovery is possible.

When we hope, we move from "tough love to loving well."[15]

When we hope, we assure our family member or other loved one that no matter what happens, we know there is a pathway of change waiting for them when they are ready.

Remember

Understanding addiction and recovery can help reduce barriers that people often face in seeking help. Having hope for loved ones can help foster hope within themselves.

Reflect

- What are five things that you hope for your loved one, whether they are still struggling in active addiction or in recovery?
- How can you help to foster a sense of hope around these five things?

Chapter 5

Letting Go of Labels

If I speak of myself in different ways, that is
because I look at myself in different ways.
—Michel de Montaigne

"My son is an addict."

"She is an alcoholic."

"Our family has struggled with my addict husband for years."

"My best friend is an addict in recovery."

Have you heard or maybe even used the words *addict* or *alcoholic* to refer to your loved one?

Julie Merberg, a mother whose son is in long-term, sustained recovery, writes extensively about her experience as an affected family member in her Substack newsletter, *The Opposite of Addiction*. In one of her letters, she shares about when she learned about narrative therapy, something used often in marriage and family therapy. Julie chose to go back to school to become a counselor to help other families like hers, and learning more about this approach opened her eyes to how the story she told about her son and her family impacted more than she could imagine—including how she viewed her son.

The story she told about her son? He was an addict first. Everything else, including being a son, came second. His identity became wrapped up in the actions and symptomology of his substance use disorder.

Julie shares,

> When we call someone an addict, we are pathologizing that person, making them one with a disorder. When we say that someone struggles with addiction, that separates the human from the issue—empowering the person and also their family to tackle the problem without attacking a loved one who is already suffering. Psychologically, this tweak puts everyone on the same team—against the issue. Linguistically, it erases the judgment of the person who is struggling with something.[1]

She states that when we can separate the "person from the problem," we externalize the struggle. It becomes something that is happening and not something we are intrinsically. Though our addiction or substance use challenges can be a part of us or a part of our loved one's experience, it isn't who we *are*.

A series of interviews I conducted for my role as a global researcher in the field of family recovery support and as cofounder of the Global Family Recovery Alliance was revealing. When asked about the main barrier for family members receiving the support and services they need, there was resounding agreement: stigma.

This small word with a world of hurt attached is something that I've spent over a decade studying and writing about.

Why? Because it is a significant barrier for not only people in or seeking addiction recovery, but for family members. When we are stigmatized, we are othered. We are told we don't belong and, worse, that we don't deserve belonging. We wear a "proverbial scarlet letter" that impacts not only how others perceive and relate to us but oftentimes how we see ourselves.[2]

Certainly, for those of us in or seeking recovery, the impact of stigma can run deep. Research also shows how detrimental stigma can be, with some studies showing how stigma can lead to fewer people accessing the treatment they need.

Here are other consequences of addiction stigma as outlined by the research. Those who are stigmatized

- avoid seeking help due to fear of judgment or legal consequences;
- experience social rejection and isolation, leading to feelings of loneliness and despair;
- have poor health outcomes that negatively affect physical and mental health, making recovery more difficult;
- experience obstacles in finding and maintaining employment, causing financial instability;
- receive lower-quality care due to biases and negative attitudes from health-care providers; and
- have more extreme and harsh legal penalties and consequences, rather than treatment and support.[3]

For mothers and parents, the research shows that stigma is even more prevalent, causing further damage to children and families.[4]

Dr. Asia Ashraf, a psychologist in Pakistan working in addiction treatment, shares how archaic many peoples' views on addiction and recovery are. Especially for women, the stigma is exponentially higher. In Pakistan—*today*—there are still punitive treatment measures, including beatings, deprivations like starvation, and other physically abusive practices to try to "discipline" the moral failing of addiction out of people who are struggling.

Yes, I said all of this and yes, this is still happening in our world.

Family members also experience what is termed *secondary stigma*. If our loved ones are "addicts," then something must be wrong with us too. We must share, on some level, the same moral failings that led to a life of addiction for our loved one. These feelings of *not good enough* start to settle in the heart and lead to guilt, shame, and family members not reaching out for help either.

Maybe you've experienced this: the feeling that you've done

something (or not done something) to cause your loved one's problematic substance use or addiction. Maybe you've felt this way or had friends or other family members insinuate as much.

Well, if she didn't travel so much . . .

If he was around more . . .

It all started for her when her parents got that divorce.

It's no wonder, with how soft they are as parents.

If this is you, I want to say that I'm so sorry that you've experienced this.

No one, not the affected loved one or the person in or seeking recovery, should have to experience stigma or discrimination. There is more to us than our addiction—or recovery. There is more to *us* than our loved one's story.

We Are People First

Timothy Harrington is a family transformation coach and founder of Family WellthCare Coaching. His vision is expansive, and one of his goals is to transform the landscape of substance use disorders (SUD) and mental health recovery. He works with families across the US to discover a new way to approach their affected family members, with curiosity and compassion. He is also the cofounder of Wide Wonder, a nonprofit he started with his wife after selling their home, buying an old bus, and traveling the country to eliminate stigma.[5]

Pretty radical and my kind of recovery person.

When we spoke over Zoom, he shook his California dusty-blond hair and looked like he just walked out of a surf shop. Tim told me about his passion for families and his vision, noting—like the other families I'd been talking to—what an insidious role stigma plays in the dysfunction of not only the family system but the community as well.

He shares that "stigma is the number one barrier. It gets in the way of everything."

Although there is widespread agreement that families need to be a part of the recovery process, the type of support available and how it is provided does not measure up, according to Tim. What will help is a more integrated approach that reduces stigma and encourages positive change. To foster deep and lasting connection and healing, both our loved ones and family members need to move beyond labels.

When Tim works with families in his coaching business, he shares that a main focus is reframing. "It's always trying to sort of reframe the conversation so that people feel like they can connect, because stigma is a barrier to connection." When he meets a family and they introduce "the addict," he knows his work is beginning. He doesn't want to meet people based on a label.

We don't introduce ourselves or loved ones as "the diabetic, the cancer survivor, the heart disease sufferer."

We are people first.

Vulgar Grace

Outside of my small town in rural East Tennessee, one church community is actively involved in recovery ministry. One afternoon, the program director, Matt Holder, called me to share something about a mobile home park only about five miles outside our town limits.

"They've stopped responding," he said, exasperated.

"Who?" I asked, although I feared I already knew the answer.

"The paramedics."

This particular mobile home park had a series of overdose events and calls to local first responders. Then, someone along the chain of command instructed them to stop going for the overdose calls.

Because of this, people likely died.

This church responded. The ministry loaded up volunteers in

a couple of vans, brought naloxone (the lifesaving opioid overdose reversal medication), and went door-to-door at the mobile home park. They talked to people who were hurting, talked to people who were experiencing the systemic effects of stigma. Not only internal feelings of shame and worthlessness because of their substance use disorder but an external structuring of support—or in this case, lack of lifesaving support. Stigma can kill.

How many people lost their lives and the opportunity to get well in recovery all because stigmatizing beliefs and attitudes turned into harmful actions?

I'll never forget what Matt shared with me later about what the pastor's wife at the time had said after hearing about this outpouring of love and support for this neglected and harmed community: "This is the kind of work Jesus would do."

It wasn't flashy. No social media posts capturing the exchanges between people in recovery. A ragtag bunch of folks loaded into a couple of vans to pass out lifesaving medication because they knew the lifesaving power of being loved and appreciated. Not judged or condemned for any action, but welcomed.

Author and priest in recovery, Brennan Manning, shared this in his final book:

> This vulgar grace is indiscriminate compassion. It works without asking anything of us. It's not cheap. It's free, and as such will always be a banana peel for the Orthodox foot and a fairy tale for the grown-up sensibility. Grace is sufficient even though we huff and puff with all our might to try to find something or someone it cannot cover. Grace is enough.[6]

As Jesus himself has scandalously been caught saying, "Let he who is without sin cast the first stone."[7]

In recovery circles there are no stones that can be cast around where we live, only naloxone to pass out. There are these active ways that we can be "hope with legs," combating stigma by taking action. Providing practical, evidence-based support that doesn't discriminate, label, or condemn but gives people another chance at life.

No Stigma, No Shame

There is amazing and uplifting anti-stigma work being done worldwide both inside and outside of the church. Much of it aims to, with a "vulgar grace," eradicate old notions that those of us in recovery are forever tied to the labels of "addict" or "alcoholic." Because of these organizations, people like me have come to embrace that *we are more than we've been told*.[8]

In 2023, Kentucky launched UNSHAME, a campaign to combat stigma around SUD by sharing recovery stories with communities. It is a collaborative effort between the Kentucky Opioid Response Effort and the national nonprofit Shatterproof.

By leveraging partnerships and research, the campaign reduces barriers to care and improves attitudes toward those affected by addiction. Their website hosts an amazing story catalog with stories that put a face and voice to recovery.[9] Over a one-year time frame, the campaign contributed to a 5 percent decrease in overdose deaths.

The stories feature people living healthy, meaningful, and productive lives in recovery after their struggle with opioid use disorder.

- Billy built a new family of support and a life of meaning.
- Wendy is thriving and giving back to her community.
- Jennifer found strength in a community of like-minded and healthy women.
- Lee works in recovery housing and gives back what he has gained in recovery.
- Stephanie has dedicated her life to helping others.

- Juanita, Liz, Brandi, Matt, Sam, and countless others share stories of hope and transformation.

Dr. Jason Roop is a man in recovery who went back to school to study theology. He got his doctorate and shares in his UNSHAME video that "this is not the end of the story. If you keep moving forward, if you keep putting one foot in front of the other, the next chapter of your life will become the most beautiful chapter of all."[10]

With over 472,000 adults reached in its first year and measurable reductions in stigma, UNSHAME Kentucky demonstrates the power of storytelling and the importance of reducing stigma. When we can see our loved ones outside of their choices, their illness, and their addiction or substance use disorder, our lives can be opened to the truth that recovery is possible.

Changing how we perceive and talk about our loved ones can help us connect in a new way, even if it feels like all hope is lost if your loved one is still struggling. We can choose to never stop believing. Never stop believing that our loved ones are more than an "alcoholic" or "addict."

We can also move beyond hope into action. There are practical things we can do to help lessen stigma, encourage grace, and enhance the likelihood that people in recovery—and our families—will get the help they need and sustain it over time. Maybe it is passing out naloxone with your church. Maybe it is sharing your story in a campaign. Maybe you have your own ideas about how to be a part of lessening and not spreading stigma. Maybe it is simply continuing to read this book to learn more about what you can do.

Language is powerful. Even if unintentional, labeling our loved ones can perpetuate stigma that slowly (or quickly) erodes both their and our sense of self and hope over time. If we are only the things we have done that we aren't proud of or that make us cringe, how can we find the hope on the other side of our choices or substance use disorder?

By changing how we think and talk about addiction and recovery, we can be a part of a culture of change. The following are words that promote change, instead of continuing stigma.[11]

Words That Promote Change	Words That Continue Stigma
Person with substance use disorder or person with problematic substance use	Addict, alcoholic
Person in recovery	Clean
Substance use	Substance abuse
Person experiencing substance use disorder	Drug user
Person who uses drugs	Junkie
Medication for addiction treatment or medication-assisted recovery (MAR)	Drugs
Positive drug test	Dirty

Seeing our loved ones as people first can lessen our own internal stigmas and also contribute to how they view themselves. Using language that helps bust stigma can make real strides toward helping people see themselves as worthy of love and worthy of help.

It is beautiful when we start to see ourselves as people in recovery or people seeking recovery. It is even more beautiful when our loved ones do too.

Let's pause here and acknowledge that this can be tough.

Maybe you have spoken about and thought about your loved one, whether still struggling or in recovery, in the same way for a long time.

Maybe you are afraid to trust that change has happened—is happening.

Maybe you aren't sure what to believe or how to talk because so many of the people in your support group, church, family, and workplace talk negatively or in a way that is stigmatizing.

Maybe you are confused because in some recovery circles, it's a way to greet one another. Maybe it is tough because of what your loved one has put you through, and the last thing you feel like doing is using stigma-sensitive language.

It is tough, for all of these reasons and more. But what if there is another way we can approach this, another way to understand stigma?

What If We Aren't Strangers?

As humans, we can walk into a room and immediately start creating walls, thinking, *I am not like you, and here is why.*

We construct barriers around ourselves and the "other" to separate ourselves from being what they are, whether that person is an alcoholic or addict, divorced, promiscuous, a gambler, an overeater, a gossip, or a disheveled man sitting on the curb.

Maybe, sometimes, we even separate our loved ones too.

Our child can't have a problem like that. Drugs? Alcohol? That's for old men holding a brown paper bag.

I don't understand them anymore.

I'm not like them.

How could they do this to us? To me?

Why do we do this? Why do we separate ourselves from our loved ones?

Sometimes we've been burned and it feels safer.

Sometimes our loved ones have acted in ways that still hurt when we think about it, even if they are changed, even if they are living in recovery.

Many of us also know what it feels like to be sitting on the other side of the sentiment. Hearing all around us, "*You* are not like me."

How often have we been on the other side of the glare where we are sized up? Made to feel different? With no other option than to sit on our literal or figurative curbs?

For those of us in addiction recovery, how often have we encountered stigma? Judgment instead of grace? How often have we been boxed in by how other people perceive us or connect our identities with our actions or behaviors, where who we are is wrapped up in what we do (or don't do)?

First considering and then addressing stigma is a process. It may take time to get to the place where we see our loved one not as other or different or someone separate but as so much more than their addiction or recovery or the ways they've let us down.

What if instead of seeing our loved one as different from us (whether struggling with problematic substance use, in active addiction, or in recovery), we try to find the ways we are similar?

What if we took time to learn more about how to communicate with our loved one in ways that promote a recovery-oriented mindset, in ways that are encouraging and uplifting—even if or when our loved one does not live up to our expectations?

• • • • •

When we love someone in recovery, we can look at the similarities and not the differences.

• • • • •

Even if it is tough (and I know it's tough because I'm an affected family member too), maybe it is time to believe anyway, to hope anyway, and act accordingly. We can learn from mothers like Julie and see our loved ones as people first. People with promise and bright futures, with lives ready to be lived. Even when it might be tough to hope.

Like my friends.

- Honesty, who is now the CEO of the McShin Foundation in Richmond, Virginia, where she was once a resident.

- Chekesha, who earned an honorary doctorate and wrote a book about her opioid use disorder recovery, hearing loss, and redemption story.
- Jessica, who as an affected family member started the organization called Start Healing Now to support other families.
- Heather, who worked her way to be a house manager with a driver's license, great job, and supportive "God squad."
- Matt, who became a father to two sons and two daughters and a recovery ministry director to impact countless people with his testimony and story of recovery.
- Cassidy, who is a survivor and works in countless nonprofits to share a message of hope with others.
- AJ, who mentors young professionals in recovery and has created a network of men in recovery and a fellowship of support and accountability.
- Meghann, who brings her globally recognized storytelling trainings and workshops to teach other people how to share their stories.
- Shelly, who started a counseling center that has touched the lives of thousands (including me) who then pay it forward and help others.
- Flo, a woman in recovery who became a globally recognized expert and advocate and also fanned a spark in me to be more than I knew was possible.

The list goes on and on.

We can practice separating our loved ones from their addiction—even their recovery. Seeing them as people first. We can keep a person-first approach that motivates and encourages our loved ones to keep going.

Instead of saying, "This is my son, the addict" or "This is my son, the recovering addict," try saying, "This is my son. His name is ____________. He loves writing, drawing, music, nature, books, lasagna, basketball, fantasy football, bonfires, flannel, funny TikTok videos, learning "Stairway to Heaven" riffs on the guitar, classic Nintendo, Sublime T-shirts, belly laughing, [*and more*]. He is a person seeking recovery. *He is a person* who struggles with substance misuse or addiction. He is loved."

"This is my daughter . . ."

"This is my neighbor . . ."

"This is my husband . . ."

"This is my friend . . ."

"This is me . . ."

Remember

Individuals in or seeking addiction recovery experience stigma. Family members can experience addiction stigma too.

Reflect

- Have you ever been looked down upon or stigmatized because of a loved one's addiction, substance use disorder, or recovery?
- What happened and how did it feel?

Chapter 6

Meaning in a Shared Story

> Compassion is born when we discover in the center of our own existence, not only that God is God and humans are human, but also that our neighbor really is our fellow human being.
>
> —Henri J. M. Nouwen, *The Wounded Healer*

"Are you really a heroin addict? You don't look like one. All the addicts I know have track marks on their arms and they're down begging by the Los Angeles River."[1]

Ryan Hampton tried to remain calm. In his first book, *American Fix: Inside the Opioid Addiction Crisis—and How to End It,* he talked about a revealing conversation he had with a then congressman in California.

They were meeting to discuss advocacy and how politicians can get involved. At the time Ryan was starting a movement called Mobilize Recovery, which has since spread across the recovery landscape like a brush fire. After first meeting Ryan, the congressman asked, "Are you really a heroin addict?" because he didn't know that addiction does not discriminate. It doesn't have a look or sociodemographic status or gender or skin color or religious preference or lack thereof.

I can relate to these questions. There have been innumerable times I've heard a version of the same: "You? No . . . you don't *look* like an addict or alcoholic."

Ryan explained that he preferred to be called a "person in recovery."

He went on to share about their time together:

> By the time our hour was up, David was friendlier and more interested in what I had to share. That's why it's important to show people that we are more than "addicts." David didn't expect me; he expected some skinny, strung-out guy with a paper bag. I think my humanity surprised him. It certainly opened his mind.[2]

How often does our humanity surprise others—especially those who don't understand what recovery is? This is part of why I wanted to write this book. We have a shared humanity that I think recovery can reveal in all its flawed brilliance. And addiction can impact any family in any country on any continent in the world. The science tells us this. The research tells us this. Our personal experience does too.

We have a shared story that, despite our differences, brings us closer together.

Seeing the humanity in our loved ones, however, may be especially difficult because we may remember how they were before addiction dug its claws in.

Why Us?

When we don't know how prevalent addiction and substance use is among family members and other loved ones, we can be plagued by this question: Why *our* family?

William (Bill) Stauffer is executive director of Pennsylvania Recovery Organization Alliance and another globally recognized advocate. As a "formerly young person in recovery" and in long-term, sustained recovery for over three decades, he is now a nationally recognized trainer and writer on addiction and recovery-related topics. He advocates at all levels of government for policies that support people and families in recovery.[3]

When I spoke with Bill for an interview series for the Global Family Recovery Alliance, he echoed sentiments I've heard countless families share, ones that even my own family asked in the height of my addiction and substance use: "Why? Why did this happen to our family? How can our loved one do this *to* us?"

His answer is something to consider:

> Substance use disorders are conditions that affect every kind of family in every community. There's nothing different or bad about their family if they're experiencing this. It's a common condition. The question "What's wrong with our family that this happened to us?"—this is the thing that we need to dispel. Because it's not *those* families that experience this; it's *our* families. It's families everywhere.

Bill compares substance use disorder in families to an iceberg. When we peek below the surface of our lives, like Bill suggests, what if we notice that the small piece of ice floating above the surface is in reality an iceberg of monumental proportions? With addiction, there is much more going on below the surface and behind closed doors.

The same with recovery.

What is more, this is not a lone piece of *Titanic*-sized ice; this is one in a sea of them.

After interviewing and talking with hundreds of affected family members, one of the key themes that my research highlighted was how 100 percent of the family members started on their road to healing when they connected with other families who had experienced similar things. It was through mutual support. Healing happens when we see our stories reflected back.

I've shared why opening up and sharing our stories is important, but there's another story that's important to understand and listen to: the story we tell ourselves.

The Stories We Tell Ourselves

There is an interesting therapeutic technique called narrative therapy centered on this idea of the power in stories.[4] Narrative therapy originated in the 1980s, but the power of storytelling has been known since the beginning of time.

Stories share an experience, but they can also teach or rebuke or encourage. They shape how we see ourselves and our experiences. For those of us in recovery, when our predominant story is "I'm an addict" or "I'm an alcoholic," how does that shape our worldview? Our identity? When we stigmatize ourselves by using this language (like we discussed earlier), how does that impact the stories we tell ourselves about how we can move forward in recovery? How we can change our lives?

You may have shared a story like this in the past: "Our family has been destroyed by addiction."

This is a powerful, tragic statement that carries too much truth for too many of us. I've heard countless family members talk about how their lives have been upended by their loved ones' fall into the depths of addiction. Some families have been torn apart by overdose death.

Yet this is also true: I've heard family members talk about the transformation of a loved one. The way the light comes back in their eyes. You've likely heard it, too, and maybe long for it.

"Our family is whole again."

"Our daughter is back."

"Our son is in recovery."

"Although we have struggled for years with our daughter's substance use

disorder, we are resilient. We keep showing up. We keep trying to learn new ways to support her and *maintain our sanity."*

We can reframe and "re-story" our experiences so that they carry new meaning with them—even hope.[5] As principles of narrative therapy suggest, we can rewrite the script of storylines that emphasize only mistakes and the symptoms of our substance use disorder. We can broaden our perspective by focusing on empowering storylines and move toward a healthy narrative that shines a light on the possibility of wholeness.[6] Nothing we have done can separate us from this reality. This is the real story.

Telling a New Story

The room felt electric.

Scarves and linens and manicured nails in a rainbow of pinks, turquoise, corals, and yellows. Eyeglasses like butterflies: varied colors and shapes and sizes. Women laughing and tearing up and hugging and hungry for connection.

Never had I been in a room of women so laid bare and loving it—a beautiful tapestry of experiences and ages and histories and desires. Women hurt by trauma and addiction yet so ready for more from life. They were walking reminders that *we are more*. They were rowdy and receptive, with unusually open hands to the truth that they were gathered because they were sober and loved it.

"Do you know what it feels like to be in recovery and love your new life?"

"It's *amazing*!"

The organization, called Women for Sobriety, has been around for decades. It was created by a woman in the 1970s who wanted an alternative support system than what was predominantly offered at the time.

Decades ago we did not have a list of recovery support options like a Cheesecake Factory menu: harm reduction, 12-step, faith-based, and so on. Especially for women. So a woman did what women often do: The resource did not exist, so she built it.

Women for Sobriety was born out of a desire for something different. Though I connect with other pathways, too, and talk openly about my faith, I can connect with that. So many times over my recovery journey (and even times recently) I've said, "I want something different. I am ready for more."

At the conference I discussed my book about trauma recovery. We laughed, we cried (including me), and there were shouts, claps, hugs, and yeses. I jokingly asked for a tissue from the room full of women, and of course many had fresh Kleenex or a crumply napkin to share.

Among friends, I shared about my experiences in early recovery when I realized that I was ready to go deeper with my healing. Things started happening that were pointing me toward a new story.

As one woman at the conference shared, "I realized after hearing you that I'm ready to take my recovery deeper. I'm ready for more."

My dear friend Meghann Perry hosted and facilitated the conference. She participates in the International Women's Day event that I host yearly, and she is part of the reason the event was so electric. She trains people in recovery, speakers, organizations, and others on how to tell meaningful and impactful stories. Trained in theater and recovery coaching, she brings something unique to recovery advocacy and support.

During one of her talks at the conference, she introduced the concept of "re-storying." "We can take our stories and re-story them. We can change the narrative. We can take what happened to us or maybe an old story that we've been telling ourselves, and we can share it in a new way."

Reframe.

Renew.

Reinvent.

We can outgrow our old stories.

I've outgrown so much in my life: people, places, things, actions, behaviors, stories. Old stories that are scratchy, like an old wool sweater that doesn't fit. Old stories that don't work for me anymore.

At this conference, I was lovingly reminded that we can begin telling new stories. We can re-story.

Have you outgrown an old story about your family, about recovery, or about your loved one? Maybe it's time to think about re-storying your experience. It might be time to discover where we can connect with one another's stories.

• • • • •

When we love someone in recovery, we can remember that our loved ones are writing a new story.

• • • • •

There are innumerable pathways of recovery for our loved ones, and there are countless groups and programs and meetings and supports for affected family members and loved ones to connect around shared stories of trauma and addiction and also around joyful stories of recovery. It is in this sharing of stories we learn we are like those around us. We are more alike than we are different. And importantly, we can promote change through communication and conversation.

A part of connecting with our stories is sharing them through language. It is in the shared language of mutual love and support that true healing can bloom. It is also through the process of storytelling that people like Ryan Hampton can talk about recovery and shine a light for people who still hold stigmatizing or even discriminating views.

Talk the Talk

Telling our stories of recovery, whether we are family members or people in addiction recovery ourselves, is part of the story. To tell stories, to find meaning and connection with the storyteller, we need to know how to communicate. How we talk to our loved ones matters.

Those of us who have been through the trenches with our families know how important communication is. Rarely do I recall a "positive reinforcement" approach from my family members when I was struggling as a teen or young adult, but I don't fault them. They didn't have the tools or the vocabulary. In the 1990s, society didn't either. Culturally, we didn't even know where to look, let alone know what to say.

I've heard so many family members struggle with finding the right thing to say.

"How do I talk to him when he is high? Should I even talk to him?"

"The trust is gone. When she speaks, I don't know if I can believe her."

"He's been to treatment six times. What can I say *this time* that will make any difference at all?"

"They are in recovery now, but I have no idea how to talk about *that*."

Maybe you've tried lecturing, you've tried tough love, you've tried veiled threats or even punishments: taking away the cars, the keys, the financial support, the holidays.

Maybe you've tried going to meetings with them, listening, reading books on recovery, all with the end result of continuing to feel separated by your loved one's experience.

I love what writer in recovery Anne Lamott shares in her book *Somehow: Thoughts on Love*: "Sometimes the only way you can deliver truth to a loved one is to start from deep inside, let it rise up through the chest and out the mouth, and then waft downward to the earth, a rug, a lap."[7]

To me this quote says this: I can take the pressure off myself to say or even do the right thing. When we love someone, the right words may falter or fumble, but from deep in the heart we can speak healing words if we know what they are and how to say them.

We can trust that our love can cover a multitude of wrongs. Perhaps by tapping into the place where the love of our family member was born, an eternal help is available to us. We are not alone in our stories, and we are not alone in the sharing of our thoughts and feelings to our loved ones, whether we believe in eternal help or not.

We can also take heart that by listening to our loved one's stories and experience, or perhaps those of other people in or seeking recovery, we will find new meaning in our shared stories. Perhaps even a connection we didn't know was there. But our stories don't have to be perfect, nor does the way we communicate, although we can work to learn more about how to communicate effectively with our loved ones (more on that later).

As we shared earlier, we can help our loved ones by eliminating stigmatizing language from the way we talk about them and about substance use disorder or addiction. In fact, there are some folks who think even using the word *addiction* is stigmatizing. For simplicity's sake, I've chosen to use it, sometimes interchanged with *substance use disorder*, but it proves an important point: How we talk about addiction or substance use disorder and our loved ones matters. The stories we tell matter.

Remember

When recovery is shared, hope multiplies. We can find renewed hope when we connect over the similarities and differences in our recovery stories.

Reflect

- Do you have mentors, friends, or colleagues who have impacted your story by sharing theirs?
- How does this help you understand your loved one's recovery journey in a better way?

PART 3

recovery is wellness

Chapter 7

Beyond Sober

Do you not know that in a race all the runners run, but only one receives the prize? So run that you may obtain it.
—1 Corinthians 9:24 ESV

Scott was eleven years old when he started using drugs and alcohol and quickly spiraled into a world and identity centered on substance use.[1] Throughout his twenties he continued to use, his physical health deteriorating and his sense of purpose stunted. Plagued by paranoia and fear, he came to a breaking point when he realized he had to do something different if he wanted to survive. He shares,

> I wanted to change my life but didn't know how. I was always drawn to the idea of doing something physical and being outdoors, so I went to an outdoor equipment store and bought a GORE-TEX jacket. Walking out, I saw an ice climbing brochure with a guy hanging off this massive ice cliff, and I thought, *That's the craziest thing I've ever seen.*
>
> I stayed sober through a Friday night so I could go climbing on Saturday. The guide climbed up the cliff effortlessly, and then I struggled my way up. I was sweating. My arms got pumped.

> I could barely hold on to the ice axes. My shirt was riding up, and my belly was on the ice. It was just like my life, because I was struggling at the time. But a seed was planted, and I thought maybe someday I could climb like him. It gave me something to aspire to, so I'd stay sober on the weekends to climb.[2]

Scott discovered one of the dimensions of a healthy recovery and he didn't even know it. He became inspired by a life of physical wellness, stretching beyond his limits. Setting physical goals and climbing toward them. His family and friends started to notice that what was helping Scott maintain his recovery and get healthier wasn't just quitting using substances. It was adding healthy actions to his life.

It's a Marathon, Not a Sprint

I experienced something similar when I signed up for my first half marathon. Having enjoyed long-distance running in track and then cross-country for a year before addiction stole away any of my more wholesome interests, I knew the feeling that came from crossing a finish line. A rush of adrenaline that could beat a cocaine high any day. It was exhilarating.

A couple of years into recovery, I realized I could run again.

I realized that there were so many things that I could do again.

Be on time at my job.

Pay bills.

Drive a car (with a license).

Call my parents.

Be a friend.

Take a deep breath.

I laced up a pair of fresh shoes, the soles still vibrant with color, waiting to be worn. My black Lab (RIP Mo) panting happily beside me, setting the pace. The soft earth of a nearby country park cradling each step. In late summer monarch butterflies rested on milkweed as I flew by. In autumn the crunch of fresh leaves mixed with the surprisingly fresh smell of decay. Winter meant breathing out little clouds, eyelashes collecting ice. Then spring again, and the cycle continued as the buds burst forth from the earth, reminding me as I ran by that there were so many reasons to be alive. To be sober.

Running was something that I started like Scott started mountain climbing. It was a physical action that helped my body remember what it was like to move again. Breathe again. Feel tired again (naturally). Feel good again (without substances). It was a coming home to myself, my body, a coming down to earth. And it felt good.

When I signed up for a half marathon, I researched how to train for one. I found an eight-week training plan that helped me start with short distances and gradually add distance. There were short-run days (that grew in mileage as the weeks went on) and long-run days that took me all the way to 10 miles a week before the 13.1-mile race.

I remember it felt so good to have a plan, to be working toward goals. I had forgotten how much of a "goal gal" I am. Working and then attaining something has always been a motivator for me. I love the challenge to push myself beyond what I think I'm capable of. Recovery gave me back some of these parts of myself that had been sleeping for years.

The day of the half marathon, I was nervous. It wasn't just me and Mo anymore. I parked, spit out my Nicorette gum (I was still trying to quit nicotine at that time), and walked to the registration table. Decked out in my white baseball hat, zipped-up long-sleeve Nike pullover, and running shorts, I might have looked like your average racer. But what the people around me didn't know was that training for this race was saving my life. It was giving me not only a goal to work toward but a way to heal from much of what I'd put my body, mind, and spirit through. It wasn't only helping me abstain from using drugs or alcohol; it was helping heal the symptoms of my trauma, like anxiety and high cortisol levels, that led to my substance use in the first place.

I don't think it's a coincidence that in ancient texts, including the Bible, running is a metaphor for endurance and living. Here are a few of the verses that mention running.[3]

- **1 Corinthians 9:24:** Do you not know that in a race all the runners run, but only one receives the prize? So run that you may obtain it.
- **Isaiah 40:31:** But they who wait for the LORD shall renew their strength; they shall mount up with wings like eagles; they shall run and not be weary; they shall walk and not faint.
- **Hebrews 12:1:** Therefore, since we are surrounded by so great a cloud of witnesses, let us also lay aside every weight, and sin which clings so closely, and let us run with endurance the race that is set before us.
- **2 Timothy 4:7:** I have fought the good fight, I have finished the race, I have kept the faith.
- **Galatians 5:7:** You were running well. Who hindered you from obeying the truth?
- **Psalm 119:32:** I will run in the way of your commandments when you enlarge my heart!

In ancient times running wasn't something you did to shed the baby weight and fit in with your active moms' group or release steam. It was a matter of survival. In Greco-Roman times, quick feet carried news of military victory or escape from predators. Remember, there were no cell phones, cars, planes, or shotguns. Being able to move quickly was paramount to survival.

In fact, a soldier from Greece named Pheidippides is the father of our modern-day marathon (26.2 miles).[4] He ran from a city called

Marathon to Athens to carry word of a military win against the Persians before he fell at the feet of his friends with no shiny blanket, Gatorade, or energy gel pack to pick him up. This run of endurance was so memorable that many today replicate his feat (likely without knowing its origins).

As I ran my first 13.1 miles, I felt the wind at my back, as they say, and joy overwhelmed me. But what was interesting is that running the race brought only a fleeting feeling of accomplishment. What really changed my life was the day in and day out (with rest days) doing the thing. Working hard. Practicing. *Running.*

It's a lot like recovery. The need to show up, "suit up," practice. Do it again and keep going, no matter the weather or season in life.

Physical activity also does something incredible to the body in terms of healing from the abuse and neglect that we put our cells through in active addiction. But don't take my word for it. Research indicates the effectiveness of physical activity and exercise in "reducing substance cravings, promoting abstinence, and improving overall well-being."[5] It can also play a role in easing the almost unbearable symptoms of withdrawal and reduce co-occurring conditions like anxiety and depression.[6]

What it does for the mind is incredible too. We now know (thanks, neuroscience) that exercise and physical activity can promote brain plasticity.[7] Remember our lesson on addiction, recovery, and the brain? This means that when we move our bodies, it helps our brains start making new connections, new pathways, new habits. What was once a narrow and well-worn path of substance use in our minds can broaden into a tree-lined path of healthy choices.

Regular exercise also enhances mood, helps anxiety and depression, improves sleep, and promotes concentration and learning. This is especially important considering that, for most of us, substance use is about more than getting high or having fun. For most of us who have experienced addiction, it stops being fun early on, to our disappointment (a little recovery humor for you).

When we work out outside, the benefits outside only increase. There is a whole phenomenon in Japanese culture called *shinrin-yoku*, or "forest bathing." For centuries a walk in the woods was deemed a healthy practice, one that revitalizes body and mind. In the last decade empirical research backs up what people for generations have known all over the globe. Being in creation is healing on so many levels.[8] It helps people with chronic conditions by improving their cardiovascular heath and reducing stress along with boosting immunity and enhancing mental health.

For decades and in many circles yet today, it is proposed that once someone stops using drugs or alcohol, problems and their trailing consequences will stop too. This implies that recovery will happen simply with abstinence, which isn't true. This is critical for loved ones to understand.

So why all the talk of climbing, forest bathing, or even our lesson on running?

Research points to the relationship between substance use and trauma or post-traumatic stress disorder and a complex interplay between these mental health challenges. There is often more going on under the surface of addiction.[9] We often hear in recovery spaces that our substance use is but a symptom of a greater issue: co-occurring anxiety, depression, obsessive-compulsive disorder, and ADHD—the list goes on. You are likely familiar with this part of how addiction impacts your family member. Perhaps their struggles, too, did not begin with out-of-control use. Maybe they started with depression as a kid. Maybe that resulted from something that happened to them or in their life earlier on.

For adolescents who initiate substance use, there is a greater likelihood of developing a substance use disorder as an adult. Women have unique challenges and biological risk factors. The reasons go on and on for why treating addiction and problematic substance use holistically, including focusing on physical activity, is important.

When you love someone in recovery, remember that just as addiction is about more than substance use, recovery is about more than sobriety.

Our recoveries can include things like forest bathing, hiking, running, climbing, therapeutic wilderness excursions (offered by a licensed treatment program or peer support group), gardening, and more. There are innumerable ways to exercise and move our bodies in our homes, in a forest, or in a recovery community center. What is almost as helpful as exercise for those of us in recovery is having our loved ones join us in this practice.

Want to Go for a Walk?

Understanding recovery involves learning that, for many of us, physical wellness is an important element. Supporting our loved one may mean joining them for a walk outside, going for a run, or maybe even trying a mountain climb. Encouraging exercise, including outdoor exercise, can be an integral part of the recovery road.

Some of my fondest memories of my first recovery community in Madison, Wisconsin, involved going on hikes around the lake or on a soft gravel path called Pheasant Branch Conservancy, where the cranes like to migrate as a pit stop on their way south for the winter. I remember hearing fifty crane calls, taking in the scent of the large oaks, kicking acorns out of the path, saying hello to the families passing by, feeling the first snow on my eyelashes, and getting caught in the rain.

Not only did I discover what movement did for my recovery but I wanted to share it with my friends. Scott Strode felt the same.

> The first time I went running, I was still smoking cigarettes and I had just gotten sober. I ran 300 yards and had to walk home huffing and puffing. But I fell in love with endurance sports.
>
> I went from falling my way up an ice climb to being a pretty confident climber. I started climbing bigger mountains, and I began dreaming of going to the Himalayas and the Andes. In the decade after getting sober, thanks to my recovery, I was able to do those things.[10]

But it wasn't just about him, as most of us who sustain recovery learn over time. Scott was able to share what he learned and to "carry the message" that physical activity is healing.

> I started by putting flyers up in supermarkets and coffee shops that said "climbing on Friday night," and I'd buy a couple punch passes at the climbing gym and stand outside.
>
> I was super bummed the first couple weeks when no one came. But one night, a guy showed up—his name was Barry. And then another came, and another, and today there are half a million people who are served by The Phoenix.[11]

His advice is simple: Move your body five days a week. He says this can be a brief walk with your family or a more intense and regimented fitness program. Move and you will gain more than you can imagine.

Scott's organization, called The Phoenix, is all about active community. Health and wellness is so much more than sobriety. The Phoenix's mission is to fight social isolation with healthy activities. Go to their website to see an interactive map with events listed all over the country, from sledding to rock climbing to open gym or yoga.

It takes courage to admit that the recovery journey is about more than sobriety. When we understand this, it opens us up to the reality that there are many ways to address addiction and to remain in long-term, sustained recovery. There are also many types of physical activities that we can encourage or support as family members or loved ones.

It takes courage to walk (or run) alongside our loved ones as they sometimes stumble along a path toward recovery. It takes bravery to admit that we might not know it all. We need to pull up a chair—or better, go for a walk—and listen to the stories being shared around us. Stories like Scott's, of physical activity, movement, healing, and ultimately finding purpose in movement and sharing that recovery is physical wellness too. We can thrive, recover, and live a life that shows us how recovery is so much more than we think.

Remember

Everyone can benefit from living a healthy lifestyle, and recovery is about physical wellness too.

Reflect

- How has your loved one's physical health changed since recovery?
- How can you model healthy lifestyle changes (or how does your loved one model this for you)?

Chapter 8

Mental Health Is the Key

We do not think ourselves into new ways of living,
we live ourselves into new ways of thinking.
—Richard Rohr

"I wore the same pair of socks and shoes for days in a meth binge and developed a fungus on my feet."

"My teeth turned black and started falling out, rotting because of lack of care."

"I was so thin, nothing fit because I forgot to eat. Wasn't hungry."

"I kept vampire hours, waking up as the sun set and falling asleep—or trying to—as the sun rose."

"My anxiety was through the roof. I didn't know how to relax anymore."

"Fear overwhelmed me. I didn't think I'd make it, and I was scared to die."

When we are in active addiction, we forget about wellness basics. Not only for our physical health but our mental health too. These quotes do not reflect the unusual or out of the ordinary for people in or seeking recovery. Though they may be startling to you, they can be a common experience. In active addiction we can forget that one of the most important things is caring for our bodies and minds.

But in recovery, like Scott Strode and his amazing organization,

The Phoenix, we learn that recovery is more than putting the substances down. It is finding what to pick up instead. Maybe it is a guitar. Maybe a pen. Maybe, like Scott, mountain climbing gear and then tax-exempt status for an organization that serves millions. It is physical health and discovering ways to move our bodies in a healthy way to promote joy and an elastic brain. It is also equally mental health. To tend the garden that is our recovery and to support our loved ones, we must understand that our minds, like our bodies, need support.

This Can Be Cured, Right?

A couple of years into my recovery, the anxiety became so bad that I started seeing a therapist again regularly. I started medication. I prayed. I read my Bible. I went to a small group. I went to my recovery meetings. I did all the things that I thought were going to cure me—or at least make the anxiety less debilitating. There were even people (well-meaning people) in my life who said things like "You just need to pray more," "You need to trust God more," and "You are living in fear, not faith."

This is what I heard: "You are the problem."

When struggling with anxiety in early recovery, it felt something like this:

Tunnel vision.

Heart out of rhythm.

Mouth drying out.

Hands and feet tingling, then numb.

Mind set on one thing: *I am going to die. This is never going to end.*

Have you ever experienced anxiety? You can't sleep or settle your racing thoughts. Or worse, it gets in the way of your daily life. For many of us in or seeking recovery, anxiety, depression, or other mental health challenges are commonplace.[1]

I didn't know at the time, but I would later be diagnosed with generalized anxiety disorder and post-traumatic stress disorder (anxiety is one of its main symptoms).

"Just pray more. Or just [fill in the blank] more." Have you had people tell you this related to your mental health? Or perhaps related to your loved one in or seeking recovery?

From these often-well-meaning critiques, this can be inferred: "It's my fault." Or worse, "I'm the only one who can fix it."

No matter if it is your loved one who is struggling or if you are facing anxiety or an anxiety disorder, you are not alone. Anxiety disorders rank as the most prevalent mental health conditions in the United States, impacting over 40 million adults, which constitutes 19.1 percent of the population.[2] The most frequently occurring anxiety disorder in the US is generalized anxiety disorder, affecting 6.8 million adults.

Younger individuals, particularly those between eighteen and twenty-four years old, are more prone to experiencing symptoms of anxiety, with nearly half reporting either depressive disorder or anxiety symptoms.[3] And women are more than twice as likely as men to grapple with an anxiety disorder.[4] Despite anxiety disorders being highly treatable, more than 60 percent of individuals affected do not seek treatment.[5]

In many ways anxiety is normal. Some may argue that we are living in an anxiety-inducing world, more so now than ever. Our primordial selves have the fight-or-flight responses kicking in because we are human. We are created to self-preserve. To endure.

Did you know that for those of us in addiction recovery, the rates of mental health conditions like anxiety are even higher? Not only this, but there is a whole array of co-occurring conditions that impact the way we recover as individuals and as family members.

For me and countless others, anxiety and depression are two rocks that weigh us down or resurface when life gets challenging or something triggers us. Sometimes when we are least expecting it.[6]

When I recently surveyed thousands of people in my email community, the number one thing they wanted to learn more about was mental health and recovery, including how to address anxiety and depression. This points to the universal experience of struggling with mental health and wanting to learn how to heal.

For years my own diagnoses bounced back and forth between anxiety and depression—specifically, these two mental health challenges to extremes. Let's say it was like living on a stormy, unpredictable sea.

What I did learn was that these two conditions were the result of not only brain chemistry and wiring that had been handed down to me genetically but also the response my body and mind had to the trauma I had experienced. Take away the substances (in many ways, my unhealthy attempt to self-medicate), and my mental state was even more unstable.

Dr. Malasri Chaudhery-Malgeri, chief clinical officer and advisory board member of Recovery.com, shares,

> Unresolved trauma can dramatically warp the brain's architecture, leading to profound shifts in how we manage stress and emotions. In this altered state, where anxiety holds sway and emotions teeter out of control, substances often masquerade as shelters from the storm. Individuals aren't chasing a high; they're seeking an escape hatch from relentless psychological pain. This isn't about pleasure—it's about survival, an attempt to soften the jagged edges of trauma that cut deep and constantly.[7]

This is what many of us in or seeking recovery understand in our bones. Substance use and addiction is a symptom of more going on beneath the surface. And for many of us, using substances is our way to cope with mental health challenges. Although it may be tough, you might need to hear this: Your loved one's struggle with addiction or problematic substance use may be related to the trauma they experienced and the related mental health conditions that accompany it.

Instead of asking, "What's wrong with you?" perhaps instead we can ask, "What happened?"

This might hurt your heart.

I feel this deeply with you.

You don't want your loved one to struggle with addiction, and you definitely don't want to hear there may be underlying reasons related to their mental health and possibly trauma they experienced. But this is the truth, and in order to get to the root, we must expose it. We have to dig deep.

The encouraging part of this is that your loved one is not alone in this. They are not unusual. It is normal to have a response to difficult circumstances. Talk to any treatment center, jail, or recovery home. Nearly 90 percent of people in recovery like me have experienced trauma.* Many of us have diagnosed—or undiagnosed—post-traumatic stress disorder.

I asked my friend Jonathon M. Seidl, author of *Confessions of a Christian Alcoholic* as well as a bestselling book on anxiety, for his thoughts on mental health and recovery. Here is what he shared.

What was it like to experience anxiety or other related mental health challenges? How did this connect with your substance use?

I never realized how deep-rooted my anxiety and OCD were. In fact, I thought I had done all the work that needed to be done. Sure, I knew that the anxiety and OCD would be an ongoing battle, but I thought they had peaked and now I was equipped to deal with them. I was wrong. What I didn't realize was that the hardest parts of my life were still ahead of me. And when I experienced those, the mental health that I thought was manageable quickly became unmanageable. That triggered a deep-seated coping mechanism that I had always struggled with: I became an alcoholic.

* I'd like to suggest that perhaps 100 percent of us today have experienced varying degrees of trauma.

How does focus on your mental health connect with your recovery journey?

What I realized once I finally admitted I had a drinking problem is that unless I got to the root of why I drank, I would just be playing a game of whack-a-mole my entire life. When my mental health took a dive in the worst way I had ever experienced, I finally fully understood that it wasn't even the mental health I needed to treat—there were things even deeper than that.

Is there anything you think is helpful for family members to understand, like your wife or kids, about your mental health and recovery journey?

I believe strongly that addiction is a multiheaded beast. Some like to say it's all physical. I think they're wrong. Others like to say it's all spiritual. I think they're wrong too. It's both. And because of that, it makes it hard to fully understand. I believe there are deep-seated emotional and spiritual issues at the heart of me wanting to escape through alcohol. But I also know that the substance itself takes over and my physical body can't stop; it craves it. So what does that mean? Well, I think for families they have to understand that the approach to helping and healing is not one-size-fits-all and has to be multifaceted. You know what else that means? It's going to require grace. Lots and lots of grace.

In our conversation together, Jon reveals deeper-seated issues, the "multiheaded beast." Addiction is only one part of what is going on, and as family members and loved ones, it can help us to understand a more holistic picture.

Whatever mental health condition your loved one (or perhaps you?) are carrying, I'd like to encourage you with this: Things can get better. We can change. Right down to the way our brains are wired.

We can heal.

The brain is resilient and powerful, like the spirit. Importantly, our actions—healthy actions—can rewire our brains even if anxiety and depression are woven into our DNA.

When mental health challenges like anxiety or depression or obsessive-compulsive disorder or ADHD creep in (again, a common response), this only adds to the pressure to be "cured" from our addiction—and the guilt that follows when we are not.

When our loved ones get sober or find recovery, we don't need to be surprised if other things resurface, as Jon shares, like a game of whack-a-mole. Address one and another pops up in its place. Addiction can mask underlying issues and mental health challenges. What's amazing is recovery can address not only substance use but mental health too.

The good news is we can do things to support our loved one's mental health. We can encourage healthy and positive actions. We can "create a nurturing, judgment-free space and advocate for professional intervention without stigma."[8] We can support the whole of who our loved one is, seeing beyond a one-dimensional view of their struggles into a broader picture of who they are as humans having experienced hard things, humans trying to cope, humans trying to get by. After we learn more we can work together to address our own mental health and well-being. We can act to not only *feel* comfortable in our skin but *be* comfortable in our skin: at peace and at ease.

Recovery Practices for Mental Health

Recovery includes building a resilient and healthy mind. I love the phrase "renewing the mind" because it implies a reboot. Have you ever wiped a computer's hard drive clean? I haven't because I'm not tech savvy (my husband is), but doing so reminds me of the verse in Romans 12:2 that talks about the renewing of the mind: "Do not be conformed to this world, but be transformed by the renewal of your mind, that by testing you may discern what is the will of God, what is good and acceptable and perfect" (ESV). A "mind renewed by truth experiences liberation."[9] What a freeing thought.

We do not have to let mental health challenges like anxiety weigh us down or lead us down a path of recurring self-medication, problematic substance use, or addiction. We can focus on supporting our loved one's healing from the deeper layers of mental health challenges during the recovery process. We might find that we are on our own journey too.

Now, let's consider three important ways that we can work to renew or reset our own mental health. This might be helpful information for your loved one or might be helpful for you to practice in your own life as well.

Rethink Your Thinking

"Your best thinking got you here," my first sponsor in 12-step recovery told me when I shared that I was thinking about dating a guy before I had one year in sobriety. "And if our best thinking got us here, do you think we should lean on our own understanding?"

It was a good question, and one of many that I'd learn to ask myself in early recovery.

For family members, our thinking can be equally as muddy. We've been worried and possibly stressed to the max over our loved one's struggle, or perhaps we are confused by their newfound recovery and change.

We can also address our thinking (which I'll talk more about in the last section of the book). Part of why I included the information on stigma and the science of addiction and recovery early in this book is to help us *think* about addiction in a new way. Armed with new information, we can see the world and our loved ones with compassion instead of judgment and with love instead of resentment. What's more, we can choose the way we think. We don't have to succumb to the destructive whims of our anxious or harmful thoughts. We can take them captive, examine them, reframe them, or remove them.[10]

• • • • •

When we love someone in recovery, we can enhance our understanding about what recovery is and change the way we think about it.

• • • • •

I love this saying: "How you think about a problem is the first step to a solution and the first thing you can change."[11] What are helpful ways to reframe our thinking related to our loved one's journey?

To help us do this, I want to share information synthesized from decades of research on family recovery from the invaluable resource *Beyond Addiction: How Science and Kindness Help People Change.* The following provides a glimpse of hope on the horizon as we walk through the rough road of addiction or the uncertain one of recovery. These are all examples of how we can rethink what we know. Hopefully this information can also help to ease our own anxieties or fears about how we can support our loved ones.

Old Thought: There is nothing we can do.

New Thought: *Families can help their loved ones.* Yes, it is true. Families matter. Research consistently points to the truth that when families are involved, their loved one is more likely to engage in treatment and recovery support services—and maintain recovery.

Old Thought: I don't have time to take care of myself.

New Thought: *Helping ourselves helps them too.* Self-care for family members impacted by addiction is key. Whether we buy into the lavender salt baths or seek support from other family members with lived experience, taking care of ourselves will model self-care to our loved ones and help us show up in healthier ways.

Old Thought: We are the only ones who deal with addiction in our family.

New Thought: *Addiction is normal.* Substance use and substance use disorders impact almost all families today. With the advent of horrific synthetic opioids, legalizing substances that used to land us in jail, vape pens (Lord, have mercy), and an ongoing alcohol crisis, we don't have to feel in the minority for dealing with the aftermath of addiction or supporting a loved one in recovery. Chances are those who *don't* go through this are the odd ones out these days.

Old Thought: My loved one is an addict or alcoholic.

New Thought: *My loved one is a person first.* Changing the way we talk about our loved ones goes a long way in helping us understand them. When we stop seeing our loved one as *the addict* or *the alcoholic*, we can focus on their personhood and not one of the many characteristics about them. Talking in non-stigmatizing ways about our loved one can promote a more empathetic and compassionate view of our loved ones.

Old Thought: They need treatment once and then they will be cured.

New Thought: *Treatment is one of many ways to get better.* Treatment is no longer seen as the only way to begin or sustain lasting change, although this is a key part of healing for many people seeking recovery. Understanding different levels of care in treatment and learning about the many pathways of recovery and types of recovery support services for maintaining long-term health are integral to supporting our loved ones.

Old Thought: If they aren't ready to change now, they will never be.

New Thought: *Resistance to change is normal.* Ask anyone who has tried to go on a diet. When your significant other orders a piece of chocolate cake after dinner and you are left pushing around cherry tomato remains with your fork, the decision to give up sugar feels, well, ill-timed. It is normal to feel ambivalent; on the one hand change sounds great, and on the other hand keeping the status quo can seem easier. Unfortunately, in many traditional treatment settings, resistance to change or ambivalence (which can sometimes lead to a recurrence of use) has led to ineffective black-or-white thinking. Many programs end up refusing treatment for those who need it the most, with recovery homes kicking out people for using—the very reason they need support in the first place.

When we can replace new information with our old thoughts, we can be more equipped to support our loved ones in recovery. Even if they are struggling.

Notice Your Feelings

You've heard the phrase, she "wears her heart on her sleeve"? In early recovery I felt as if my heart was beating outside of my chest. Years of emotions masked by substance use were suddenly laid bare. All the terrible feelings I'd buried for years in my active addiction started bubbling up like an oil spill in the ocean. It felt as difficult to manage as a coastal cleanup. What I didn't know was that I was beginning the journey of learning how to feel—one of the most important things I've learned how to do in recovery.

One afternoon I told my therapist how I was feeling out of control. But this time it wasn't my addiction that was unmanageable. My emotions were a train off the track. I was terrified about where this train was headed.

She looked at me and said something that I wasn't expecting. Just like I was learning steps to address my addiction in community, I could do the same for the emotions. It was okay if I was overwhelmed. In fact, it was a good thing. Now that I was sober, there was something that I could do about them. It was time to take action.

"The first step is learning how to identify them," she said with a smile that annoyed me back then. "You can learn how to name your feelings."

I learned that day that naming feelings wasn't rocket science. It was simple. All I had to do was start by asking myself this simple question: What am I feeling?

In Jennie Allen's book *Untangle Your Emotions*, she explores the concept of emotions and feeling. I think this book is a game changer for the recovery community.

Why?

Because I and so many of the women I've worked with over the years have spent years imprisoned in our minds. Held captive by feelings—or in some of our cases, held captive by the unquenchable desire to run from them.

Fear.

Anger.

Resentment.

Timidity.

Despair.

Even joy or happiness.

Or maybe you can relate with the feeling of not wanting to feel at all?

What I've learned, and what Jennie so practically shares in her own book, is that when we allow ourselves to feel, when we identify our feelings, something incredible happens: We can move on from them. And in some cases, learn from them.

Jennie says, "Feelings can't be beat back, by the way. They can't be ignored or dismissed. They are trying to tell us something."[12]

Hiding from or denying feelings may work for a time, but they always come creeping back.

We can feel, then "untangle" our feelings and learn how to live a more full and free life. We can be in touch with everything: the pain, the joy, the anger, the anxiety, all of it. And while our feelings are a solitary thing, they don't have to stay locked away in our minds or hearts. We can name what we are feeling. We can sit with those feelings. And we don't have to sit with them alone.

It is important for our loved ones to understand that in recovery we learn how to identify the rainbow of emotions we are feeling. It's strange at first, and we are a bit like toddlers learning to walk. But we jump in. We figure it has to be easier than what we do when we are using. Because the thing about burying emotions is that they always come back. Just like those zombies in the music video for "Thriller." (If you are an '80s baby, you know what I'm talking about.)

The second step in the process, we learn, is sitting with our feelings. Wrestling with them. Letting ourselves cry and scream and run and flail. Let's allow ourselves to notice and feel those emotions because addiction is hard. What we have been through is tough.

As loved ones, this applies to us too. Even if our loved one is in recovery, the hard doesn't go away. We need to allow ourselves to feel all of it to get free from it.[13]

Take Positive Actions

Addressing both thinking and emotions are integral to mental well-being both for those of us in recovery and our loved ones. Part of growing in understanding for our loved ones is also recognizing that addressing mental health and wellness is not only something we do with our heads and hearts. Mental health is about *taking action*, whether that is connecting in community, seeking outside support (e.g., therapy, medications, and/or treatment), or trying something new to support your or your loved one's recovery.

We will talk more soon about the power of community, but for now I'm going to share that one of the most important actions we can take for our mental health is to connect with others.

We can learn how to think and share these thoughts with people we trust. We can practice feeling and share these feelings with other safe people. For family members, connecting with other family members who have gone through or are going through something similar can be life-giving.

While our thinking and feelings can be solitary things, they don't have to stay locked away in our minds or hearts anymore. They are about actions, about walking out this renewing of our minds in community with others.

If you are struggling today with feeling some tough things, there are a couple of actions that you can take. Name it. Sit with it. Share it. Then see what happens. In my experience, what follows is freedom.[14]

When More Support Is Necessary

There are times when more support for mental health is needed. At the end of this book is a list of helpful resources for support.* My recommendation based on my experience as a trained mental health provider is to reach out for necessary support when what you are doing is not working, when your daily life is impacted, when people you trust recommend you do so, or when your heart is prompted to. You might be feeling intense feelings like loneliness or experiencing things like intense anxiety or depression. There is no shame in reaching out for support. This might be to a therapist, family counselor, psychiatrist, psychologist, pastor, sponsor, or more. It's a sign of strength, not weakness, when we do this.

---

* Recovery.com is also a great place to start if you are looking for mental health or addiction treatment for yourself or a loved one.

As Mr. Rogers shares, "When we talk about our feelings, they become less overwhelming, less upsetting, and less scary."[15] This is sage advice for all of us.

As our family members and loved ones learn how to think, feel, and act in more healthy ways in recovery, we can also take steps toward understanding the expansiveness and depth of not only their recovery journey but ours.

Remember

Renewing the mind can be a key piece of the recovery process, both for our loved ones and for us.

Reflect

- How is tending to your mental health a priority for your family?
- Are there thought patterns you can change, emotions you can feel, or actions you can take to support your loved one (or yourself) today?

Chapter 9

Boundaries Are Brave

What if your limitations were, in
fact, your greatest gift?
—Sara Hagerty

The bills started piling up: cash advance notices, rent payments, all those past parking tickets that I'd stuffed in the glove box. Money was tight. I was still working full-time, but when most of my hard-earned money went to cigarettes, drugs, and SpaghettiOs or ramen (in that order), there was nothing left when I needed it.

One day I opened an official-looking letter and was shocked that my license had been revoked. Turns out if you don't pay parking tickets, that's what happens. Another adult lesson learned the hard way. About that same time I was in a horrible car accident that totaled my car and mangled a dear friend. I also was so behind on rent that I had to sit in court, about to be evicted. In other words, my world was falling apart. I was on the edge of the consequences of my active addiction and poor choices.

I was also at a crossroads of sorts. Looking back, it was one of those moments that could have gone both ways.

Here, I recognize the privilege I experienced for many reasons. One of the most privileged positions I found myself in was this: I was extravagantly loved.

When I didn't realize it.

When I didn't deserve it.

Even when I couldn't accept it.

My mom's first husband, Greg, was someone I have always seen as a father figure, one of those people in my life who was there when I needed him. Even after months of me not calling him, he picked up the phone with a jolly "Helloooo." After I lost my license and realized that I'd soon lose my job without being able to drive, I called Greg.

Instead of sending me a check or dropping off cash, he drove me to the DMV, waited for a couple of hours on pleather-covered, back-ache-inducing chairs, and paid the bill.

"I'll pay you back someday when I can," I said, and he smiled.

After the car accident, he helped pay for a new-to-me used car, and I said again, "Someday I will pay you back when I can."

"Okay, okay," he'd say and smile.

Now, Greg was a retired fireman who was not made of money, but what he had, he shared with those in need. Freely generous.

When I was experiencing severe anxiety after the car accident and smoking way too much cannabis, which made me super paranoid, I called him and the sound of his voice let me know I was going to be okay.

Greg loved me well, but he also had boundaries. He never gave me cash. He had high expectations of me and told me so. When I brought home less than eligible bachelors, he flat out told me I could do better. When I reeked of cigarette smoke, he reminded me of the dangers.

When I was really down and out, he was there. Giving me a hug and meeting me for lunch even though I was using again. Saying he was proud of me even when I had to go to treatment *again*.

Greg's love was extravagant and showed me how someone can love in a healthy way. But looking back now, I see how it must not have been easy. It takes courage to approach a loved one with open arms, especially after being burned. It is a brave act to love unconditionally yet set boundaries when a loved one is in active addiction or struggling in other ways.

His support is a perfect example of how *support is not enabling* and how providing for basic needs, even financial ones, can save us. Having boundaries is brave. Loving despite the risk is worth it.

You might be thinking that this all sounds great and Greg sounds like a model human being, but what is a grace-filled approach to boundaries? How can you do it?

This is a tough conversation. Boundaries aren't about learning ways to wall off our loved ones or shut them out so they will stop hurting us by their actions, nonactions, choices, or mistakes.

Let's dig into this a bit, but first, let's talk about what boundaries *aren't*. They are not

- Selfish
- Harmful
- Guilt-inducers
- Enders of relationships
- Propellers of anger

This list of what boundaries are *not* may be tough for you to read too. I've personally struggled with feelings of guilt when I set boundaries. I've had fear that people in my life will be harmed or feel that I am angry with them if I set a boundary. There are all sorts of ways that our perceptions of boundaries can be distorted, especially when we are talking about them in relation to our loved ones in or seeking addiction recovery.

To help demystify what boundaries are and how they can help us as we learn more about recovery, let's lean on the experts since (full transparency) I am still very much working on this in my own life and recovery.

What Are Boundaries?

For affected family members and loved ones, this may be the most googled phrase: "What are boundaries?" We want to set them. We want to know how to create them. We want to know what to allow and what to reject in terms of our loved one's actions. After all, we want to help them and to love them—and not lose our minds or a good night's sleep in the process.

If our loved one is on the recovery road, we want to know what boundaries we need to keep ("Is it okay to keep alcohol in the house?" "Can I invite her to my birthday party?" "Should New Year's Eve be alcohol-free if he shows up?") and what boundaries to brush away like a painted line in the sand. We want to know what we should carry for our loved ones and what we should not.

"In aiding a loved one battling substance use, we must weave compassion with clear boundaries."[1] But how?

I wish I had a magic answer for you, along with a magic wand that would share the perfect advice on boundaries and solve all your problems—*right now.* Unfortunately, I cannot do that for several reasons, including that I have struggled with boundaries all my life.

If you are still reading, you know that I am a book lover. Books I love and have been moved by are peppered in everything I share (just take a quick glance at the endnotes). Dr. Henry Cloud and Dr. John Townsend are two psychologists who study people for a living and help them with dysfunctional and boundaryless relationships. They also wrote one of the most popular self-help books of all time: *Boundaries: When to Say Yes, How to Say No to Take Control of Your Life*. I will be relating each of the examples of boundaries that they discuss in their book to supporting a loved one in or seeking recovery.

"Boundaries define us. They define *what is me and what is not me.* A boundary shows me where I end and someone else begins, leading me to a sense of ownership."[2] According to Cloud and Townsend, they involve (for all humans at any age or stage) the following actions:

1. The ability to be emotionally attached to others, yet without giving up a sense of self and one's freedom to be apart.

2. The ability to say appropriate no's to others without fear of loss of love.
3. The ability to take appropriate no's from others without withdrawing emotionally.[3]

Another important characteristic of boundaries is the ability to show up in an unconditional way.

This can be *really* tough for affected family members. I've been on the receiving end and on the side of trying to unconditionally love the person in recovery or struggling with addiction. And I've worked with countless people in or seeking recovery who are harmed by the conditional nature of love that says, "You're lovable when you behave. You aren't loveable when you don't behave."[4]

Conditional love shares that when our loved ones are "good," all is well. Love is freely given. When they are "bad" or don't live up to our expectations, desires, or wants for their life, we withhold love. When they don't make the right choices (according to us), we withhold love. When they use substances then we will withhold love, loving-kindness, or loving actions.

Okay, let's pause for a moment.

This last part is not meant to judge or condemn. I think we can all raise our hands here and acknowledge that we have not always loved in an unconditional way. We're human, after all.

Is there a way to love unconditionally *and* with boundaries? Especially when most of us fail so miserably at loving even under the best of circumstances? Cloud and Townsend assert there is a way. "Boundaries aren't inherited. They are built."[5]

To explore this more deeply, let's take a look at the examples of boundaries or the "laws of boundaries" and how those relate to addiction recovery and supporting and understanding our loved ones.*

---

* This list is synthesized from the key themes in "Ten Laws of Boundaries," chap. 5 of Henry Cloud and John Townsend, *Boundaries: When to Say Yes, How to Say No to Take Control*

- **Speaking the truth in love.** We can set loving boundaries with our words when we clearly communicate with our loved ones. For example, we can share love, care, and concern, and still clearly communicate a boundary. Speaking the truth in love can help foster responsibility. It may be uncomfortable. (Or if you are a people pleaser or the adult child of someone who struggled with substance use, like me, it may be excruciating.) But we can give care and tell the truth—even when it's tough.
- **Allowing (or not interrupting) consequences.** Natural consequences can be essential for someone in recovery to experience the full impact of their choices, helping them take responsibility for change rather than relying on loved ones to shield them. This can be tough when we do not want our loved ones to experience hurtful or hard consequences. My family, including Greg, had to set firm limits around how they supported me. Providing for my physical needs (including shelter) instead of giving me money, for example. In the same way, there can be positive consequences or outcomes that our loved ones get to experience in recovery too. New opportunities with employment, school, relationships, and giving back can all be positive experiences after walking through tough consequences.
- **Responding (not reacting).** Being in control of our emotions and actions can be a freeing way to set and maintain boundaries. Emotionally reacting out of fear, anger, frustration, confusion, or any other negative emotion can produce the opposite result that we hope for when relating to our loved ones in or seeking addiction recovery. Responding, including listening empathetically, sharing gentle feedback when the person is open to it, and making decisions based on facts (not feelings), can help us respond to our loved ones in a healthy

---

of Your Life (Zondervan, 1992), 85–105. I included information that most clearly relates to affected family members and loved ones.

way. Sometimes we need to step away and call a supportive friend, take a break or a couple deep breaths, or spend time in prayer to get a responsive, instead of reactive, perspective.

- **Promoting responsibility and controlling what we can.** Encouraging personal accountability in recovery empowers individuals, while affected family members and loved ones can also take responsibility for their own boundaries, emotions, and well-being. Living in our lanes—as the common expression in recovery goes—can be freeing. Controlling what we can and letting go of what we cannot promotes personal responsibility while also leaving room for showing up to support our loved ones in healthy and compassionate ways. We cannot make choices or take action on behalf of our loved ones, but we can share positive reinforcement and praise when positive actions are taken.
- **Showing up honestly (and boldly) to take action.** Honest and direct communication helps rebuild trust in relationships strained by addiction. Having an open dialogue and encouraging honesty can help both the recovering individual and their loved ones clearly express their needs and limits. We might fear that being honest will hurt our loved one, but showing up authentically in the relationship will help to model the same type of honesty that we value. From a place of authenticity, we can then model taking healthy actions for ourselves (e.g., getting support like therapy, faith-based help, or peer connection).
- **Respect and encourage our loved one's boundaries too.** We can model healthy boundary setting and respect and honor the boundaries of our loved ones even when they are still struggling with substance use or addiction. For example, we can encourage them to express their feelings like sadness or anger (even when we don't think they *should* feel that way or have a right to feel that way because of how we feel as family members). We can also ask them to share their feelings or

express their needs or wants (again, even if we don't agree with them). Having an open, listening posture can help to disarm and give our loved ones permission to share where their hearts are. This sharing and listening is a way to say "We respect where you are coming from" and "We honor your boundary lines."

The good news is we don't have to do this perfectly to understand and support our loved ones. We can practice. We can show our loved ones support by holding and upholding boundaries, by creating fence lines that don't keep our love out but express it more fully.

In learning how to set and maintain boundaries, we can practice or train ourselves over time. Just like recovery itself, this is a marathon, not a sprint. Practice takes time. We can practice boundaries in community so that when we need to create them with our loved ones, doing so is like muscle memory. When we are under stress, tension, or confusion about our loved one's addiction recovery journey, we can respond in a healthy way by setting healthy boundaries.

Greg loved me well and taught me what it means to love despite the risk. To show up with both an open and guarded heart. Meeting basic needs and never giving up hope.

I'll never forget the look in his eyes when I handed him a check, paying him back for his help over the years. I don't think he ever expected it, but it was one of my proudest moments. I could give back what I had been so freely given.

Remember

Boundaries are a key function of loving relationships and we can work to build them.

Reflect

- How is boundary setting tough for you?
- What are specific examples of boundaries that you may need to practice setting now?

PART 4

recovery is community

Chapter 10

The Opposite of Addiction

> If you want to get warm you must stand near the fire: if you want to be wet you must get into the water. If you want joy, power, peace, eternal life, you must get close to, or even into, the thing that has them.
>
> —C. S. Lewis

"I'll go, but I just won't talk about my spouse or what we are going through as a family."

"When people ask about my son, I'll pretend he's away on a trip or out of the country. I don't want them to know he went to treatment."

"We can just stay home. It will be easier than admitting why we haven't slept in weeks."

"Let's skip the party. What if someone asks us why we aren't drinking?"

If you've found yourself unsure or even afraid to share that your loved one is struggling with addiction or in recovery, you are not alone.

We talked earlier about how family members experience addiction stigma, too, not just the person struggling with addiction. In the same way, family members need connection. Yet stigma can be something that isolates us and makes us feel like "the other" or like we don't belong. When we have loved ones who are struggling or even in recovery, many in our support structures or circles will not get it (or at least this is what we might initially feel).

Even though it is estimated that one in three American families and millions of families globally are impacted by addiction, we can still think it's only us or only our families. There is a famous TEDx Talk by Johann Hari in which he says, "The opposite of addiction isn't sobriety. The opposite of addiction is connection."[1] I'd like to remind us that connection is the opposite of loneliness too. This is true for those of us in addiction recovery *and* our family members.

What makes this tough is that we are a part of one of the loneliest generations. Cue a series of celebrities singing "We Are the World" via Zoom. Is this a triggering flashback for anyone else?

Remember those days early into the COVID-19 pandemic when we did not know how the story was going to go? Many of us were stuck in quarantine away from families and loved ones—giving birth alone, dying alone, celebrating alone, and mourning alone. More women started drinking, more teens were overcome by anxiety, and even more of us hunkered into our TikTok holes. It was a sad and lonely time. And we all had horribly long hair.

For family members impacted by addiction, many have felt isolated but not because of a pandemic. Maybe you feel isolated because you're worried that you're the only one struggling. You're scared that somehow your loved one's struggles with substance use or even their need to be in recovery is a reflection of your own failings and inadequacies.

What also makes this tough is that it's hard to admit that we need other people.

The Ratty Truth

In the 1970s psychologist Bruce K. Alexander and his colleagues challenged many of the leading beliefs about the power of addictive substances. His Rat Park experiment has become a famous example of how powerful community and connection is.[2] It has been cited by numerous addiction recovery experts and researchers (including me in my first book, *Downstairs Church*).

In the famous experiment, Alexander gave rats a choice between water and water laced with morphine. They were divided into groups, some rats being in a flourishing community with space, things for their ratty selves to do, and plenty of interaction with their rat friends. Those rats chose the water minus additives. The other rats were isolated, without the perks of Rat Park. When offered the choice of water or water plus morphine, they chose the water that impacted their brains, giving them a boost of the feel-good neurotransmitters (like dopamine and serotonin).

This experiment points to the power of connection and community in being a protective factor against substance use disorder.

Finding Your Kindred

More recent research points to the power of connection for everyone, not just those of us with addiction issues or substance use disorder.

Jeremy Nobel, a professor who teaches about loneliness and public health at Harvard T. H. Chan School of Public Health, shares, "Just like thirst is a signal that we need hydration, feeling lonely is a signal that we need human connection."[3]

We have this very human feeling that we must do it alone. The whole "pick yourself up by your bootstraps" mentality. But what if we did not have to struggle with our loved one's addiction or learn about the recovery process in isolation? What if we could lean on other families and the innumerable resources out there for our loved ones? What if we didn't have to be alone in our experience?

Kim Porter and her organization in Pennsylvania called Be a Part of the Conversation are making significant strides in supporting family recovery through a variety of innovative programs. As an affected family member, Kim knew that community and connection is a saving grace for many families struggling with addiction or trying to understand the recovery journey. She and her family experienced this firsthand during the early years of a loved one's struggle.

With a focus on education, community involvement, and comprehensive support, the efforts of her organization are making a meaningful impact on families affected by substance use disorders.

In 2011 Kim launched Parent Partnership meetings specifically designed for parents, guardians, and grandparents. These meetings are similar to Al-Anon or Nar-Anon but tailored to address the distinct challenges faced by parents and guardians. Unlike traditional 12-step programs, Parent Partnership meetings allow for cross talk and do not follow the 12-step traditions.

"We have twenty-two of those meetings happening every week. Half of those are on Zoom, and half of them are in person," explained Kim. "These meetings provide a safe space for families to share their experiences and support each other."

Kim shares that many families are in dark places when they first connect. The loneliness and isolation is damaging on many levels. "We've worked with family members who've disclosed thoughts of suicide because they feel so powerless, feel so exhausted and helpless."[4]

Recognizing the trauma experienced by family members, the organization offers specialized programs like Healing the Traumatized Family. These programs address the unique challenges faced by families and provide continuing education for treatment professionals, equipping them with essential skills like motivational interviewing.

This comprehensive approach ensures that both families and professionals are well supported in their recovery journeys. They also help families connect around shared experience. Through these programs many families learn that they are not alone. This opens the door to community when the illusion of separateness or difference is broken. "Being with other people who understand it is everything. It is just everything," says Kim.

Connecting in community is not only proven to be good for physical, mental, and spiritual health but it also helps us feel not so alone. Stigma is shattered when we sit in rooms, whether in-person or virtually, with other people who have had similar experiences.

Stephanie Duncan Smith says, "Our hearts are a muscle made in the image of God, made for connection. And there are so many ways of being kindred."[5] Maybe your being "kindred" is opening the door to that group room and sitting in a circle of chairs with other family members who are struggling.

Maybe you have lost loved ones tragically to substance use disorder, and your kindred is a grief share or providing peer support to families so that they can muster the strength to keep going when life is overwhelming and all too much. Whatever you've faced, find your kindred people who know what you've been through because they are going through it too.*

With a Little Help from Our Friends

For our loved ones and for those of us in or seeking addiction recovery, peer support and community is a key part of our healing.

Peer support is the term you may hear recovery programs, treatment providers, or therapists use. Peer support involves not just sharing knowledge or practical guidance but also sharing emotional support and practical help.[6] What is so transformative about peer support is that it involves not just a professional or academic sharing of information. Knowledge is forged in the furnace of experience.

* Organizations like Kim's are a great place to start if you are ready to stop going it alone. I also provide resources in the appendix that can help point you in the right direction.

Guidance can be trusted because it is gained through tears and sweat.

Peer support can take various forms and have different names, depending on where you live in the world. You might hear the phrase *recovery coach* or *peer support specialist* or *community navigators* or any number of other names. Many of us don't have special names or titles, but we can share helpful guidance because of what we have overcome or what we are currently working through.

In the next section of this book, we will talk about why it's important that those of us with lived experience in recovery—and affected family members—have the opportunity to share our experience through peer support and other ways.

I love what my dear friend Ann Bratton says about the importance of sharing with other family members who have been through similar life experiences. Ann lost her son Thomas to overdose in 2021 and has since moved with her grief into a newfound purpose to spread love and light to everyone she meets. Providing peer support is a lifeline for her as she continues to live and find meaning after the death of her son.

In a women's recovery meeting she co-leads, she shared, "In providing peer support, I'm returning to the land of the living. Without a reason to go on, I find it hard to continue. But today I know I can use my story to help someone else."

Research outlines the effectiveness of peer support and various peer support models, like sponsorship and traditional 12-step fellowships, though there are myriad examples. Just a few of the ways that peer support is effective include

- reduced rates of recurrence of use,
- increased treatment retention,
- improved relationships with treatment providers, and
- increased satisfaction with treatment and other types of recovery support services.

There is even specific evidence that points to special effectiveness for individuals on medication assisted recovery like MOUD, although more research is needed in this area.[7]

Did you know that what predicts the success of the therapeutic relationship or "therapeutic alliance" is trust and the quality of the relationship itself?[8] I learned this while getting my master's in social work and training as a mental health provider who could one day do therapy, and I was shocked. This rocked me to my core. It does not matter what type of therapy I learn or practice. It is the *connection* we have that makes all the difference.

This helped me believe in the power of peer support, the power of connection, even more.

Perhaps what we *know* is not as important as what we've *experienced* and how we connect with those we love.

The Helper Therapy Principle

I happened upon Henri Nouwen's *The Wounded Healer* in my twenties, and it changed my life. It helped me have a more compassionate view of my experience and see how God was helping me find purpose in the pain. The tough things I went through could be used for good, could be used to help other people. Nouwen shares, "When we become aware that we do not have to escape our pains, but that we can mobilize them into a common search for life, those very pains are transformed from expressions of despair into signs of hope."[9]

It reminds me of when Paul, in his second letter to the Corinthians, talks about the "Lord Jesus Christ, the Father of compassion and the God of all comfort, who comforts us in all our troubles, so that we can comfort those in any trouble with the comfort we ourselves receive from God."[10]

We are comforted by those who have received the comfort that we need. In the Bible this comfort comes from God. For example, the comfort that my friend Ann received after the loss of her son, she now shares with others. Because she has known the pain and experienced healing in many ways, she can now help others who are going through the same thing. This exemplifies the cyclical nature of peer support or helping, whether you believe God is in the mix or if you struggle with this thought.

The helper therapy principle describes the cyclical nature of support.

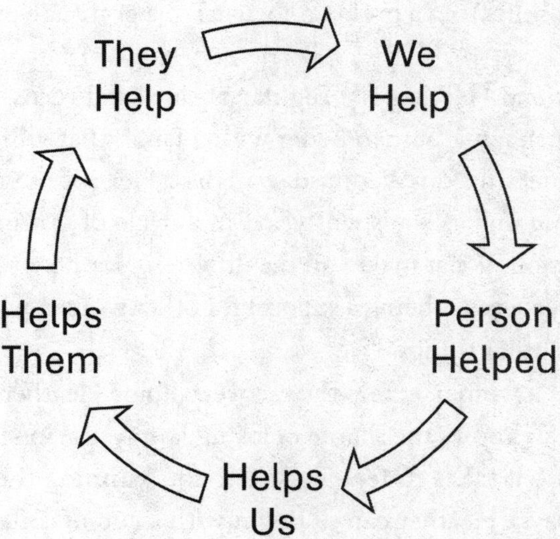

The helper therapy principle was first shared by a social scientist named Frank Riessman in a 1965 issue of the journal *Social Work*. His theory states that when an individual, the "helper," helps someone else, the person helping experiences positive benefits too. This theory is based on traditional models of mutual aid or groups like 12-step fellowships, but it is not limited to these. Riessman's research notes that connecting and helping others with similar life experiences or peer support shows positive outcomes like

- developing a stronger and more positive self-image,

- deepening commitment to a belief or stance by advocating for it (also known as "self-persuasion through persuading others"),
- enhancing personal skills and growth by teaching others,
- gaining recognition and a sense of personal worth and value through meaningful participation in the community,
- experiencing personal fulfillment and reinforcing one's well-being by serving as a role model, and
- shifting focus from personal struggles to helping others, which can shift from a problem-focused to a gratitude mind-set.

My friend Heather is a regular at our local recovery ministry and is an amazing human being with a laugh that will light up the speaker meeting on Wednesday nights. Her journey has been a challenging one as she spent years in a cycle of trauma, hardship, and addiction. What makes all the difference for her as she journeys through recovery is being a support for other women who have been through similar things.

When a woman enters the recovery home Heather lives at, and that woman knows the shame of losing family, the loneliness of jail, or the time it takes to feel joy when not "running the streets" (as Heather says), Heather can sit down with a cup of coffee and listen. She can nod in agreement to the woman sitting across from her and close her eyes and say "yes" and "amen" because she knows. She's been there too. Just like Ann. Just like you. There is power in shared connection and shared experience.

Remember

When people in recovery are connected to communities of recovery and other healthy individuals through peer support, their recoveries can flourish. Community is a key component for the loved one's healing journey too.

Reflect

- How are you connected in a community of support for family members?
- If you aren't connected, what is holding you back?

Additional Exercise

Draw three circles. In each circle write your own "circles of support."

1. Who is in your inner circle (your main people)?
2. Who comes next?
3. Who is on the outside of your circle but still available for support?
4. How does this exercise connect you to your loved one's need for community too?

Chapter 11

Healing Takes Time

If you don't like the road you're walking,
start paving another one.
—Dolly Parton

He grew up in a Christian home, went to Christian school, and had Christian friends. When he confessed to his parents one night that he used his allowance to buy cannabis, vape pens, and alcohol, his parents were shocked. When he said he had a problem with drugs and alcohol and needed help, they were wide-eyed in horror.

Their son? No!

They spent the night talking, crying, and grilling him.

"How could you?"

"When?"

"Why did you . . . ?"

"What did we do wrong?"

As the sun began to rise and purplish light filtered in through the kitchen window, the son asked what his consequences would be. He was terrified about what he knew was coming: losing his phone, car, and maybe even his ability to play on the school's sports team. Using drugs and alcohol was against the school's contract that he signed. He vowed not to do what he did.

The parents shared that they needed two weeks to think and pray about what to do next. During this time, the son was to be at home when not in class.

Naturally, the son was nervous but he was also obedient. He wasn't at the point of stealing, sneaking out, or lying like many in active addiction do to satisfy the desire to escape reality and numb feelings. He did what his parents asked. He kept his head down and his vape pen untouched.

The father and mother deliberated and ultimately decided on something that shocked even them. They decided to give him a taste of grace. There were no punishments, loss of privileges, or conversations with the school. The son was free from his debts and mistakes.

There was a moment when the son looked at his parents, the father recalls, with astonishment and then eyes beaming with love. Grace was medicine for him. Just what he needed.

Now, the father in this story (which I heard on the radio of all places) said he did not condone *no* consequences. He did not say that this was how all of these situations should be handled. But he and his wife decided after prayer and reflection that his son's actions were consequence enough. Confession demonstrated remorse and humility. What he needed now was unconditional love.

As I reflect on this story, I'm curious what happened to this boy and to his parents. Did he get the help he needed to find and sustain recovery, with understanding and support from his family along the way? Or, if he misused this free pass, did he get caught up in addiction? Were underlying issues like trauma or mental health challenges ever addressed or were they pushed away along with the pain?

Of course, I hope this was a turning point for him. I hope this taste of grace carried him into a way of life that is truly life-giving. Or even if he continued to struggle, I hope that moment in time motivated him to continue the recovery journey. I hope it is a reminder of how much he was and is loved.*

* If the son is struggling now, or if the family is struggling with his repeated attempts

What we can learn from this story is that love is one of the best ways to begin.

Have you been there? Have you thought about how often we are inclined to withhold love until we see the actions, attitudes, or behaviors we want to see? "We want action first, offering mercy only when we see a changed life."[1]

• • • • •

When we love someone in recovery, what if we choose love first, no matter what road our loved ones are on?

• • • • •

I love that this family chose love first, before the actions they wanted to see. They chose to believe in their son in that moment—perhaps just for that moment. That invitation to grace was perhaps a turning point in the boy's life and in their family's journey and an important reminder of unconditional support, not tough love.

Practice in Context

Someone asked me once why some people "get it" and stick with recovery and some people continue to "fail"—at least at first glance. Why does healing take time?

This question surprised me at the time and made me think about my own experience. And so did my answer.

"People who have the opportunity to practice change—and get positive reinforcement for this change—keep coming back."

We need to *practice* change.

It isn't one decision as much as a set of decisions, a lifestyle

---

at "getting better," or if recovery has been a hard road, I hope this book lands in that family's hands. I also hope that they don't lose hope.

change. The more time and opportunity we have to practice the life we want, the more we continue in it.

I also think back to the science of addiction and recovery, how our brains become hardwired for addiction and it takes time to untangle and rewire. It takes time to create new pathways. Especially when life feels like one long valley and our minds want to trick us into thinking the *old way* is the *easy way*.

Spoiler alert: It never is.

In many recovery circles we celebrate milestones through chips, hugs, high fives, or hearts and congrats on social media. We've got sixty days, ninety days, one year, multiple years. The longer we practice, the longer we continue to live in recovery and get positive results and reinforcements, the more likely we are to continue.

For almost seven years at an outpatient treatment center, I volunteered as a mentor. The clinic had an incredible tradition. For every annual recovery milestone, we had a recognition night. Family came. Friends showed up. Therapists and other mentors arrived, and patients at the treatment center, newly sober, watched and listened. Like an opposite roast, the person with the milestone was the center of attention, hearing nothing but love, encouragement, support, and gratitude.

I still have the card from my one-year recovery milestone, my first of many recognition nights at the treatment center. The evening started out feeling super uncomfortable, but over the hour it improved; to be loved on like that was powerful. Especially for folks like me who've felt stigma—both internal and external—for years. To be loved and showered with this love so abundantly is a gift.

Human beings need to experience the positive benefits of change to continue wanting to change until it becomes who we are. Until this new skin we are in feels like home.

For many of us in recovery (I'm raising my hand), it isn't a linear journey. There are starts and stops. Steps forward and steps backward. Even if we experience the power of being recognized, lifted up, and loved because of the changes we make.

In 12-step literature they talk about "trudging the road to happy destiny."[2] This is the recovery journey. It isn't a skip, a dance, or even a brisk walk. There are no cartwheels or jogs. It's a *trudging.* A grind.

No one wants to go for a trudge. But trust me, when you've lived in active addiction, anything sounds better than that. We recognize that we must work for it, to "work it because we are worth it," and again, this takes time. "When we accept what's hard, we don't make it harder than it is."[3] We can celebrate along the way, even through the imperfections.

The Truth About Relapse

A hard truth about recovery is that relapse or recurrence of use is often a part of the process.[4] Studies note that between 50 and 90 percent of people experience a recurrence of use; those percentages vary depending on the type of substance. Opioids, for example, have a very high relapse rate. This can be hard for affected family members and loved ones. Maybe your loved one just got out of expensive inpatient treatment—again—and had a recurrence of use. Maybe they went against their recovery home's abstinence policy and had to leave. All of these situations and more can cause additional stress for families who are already stressed to the max.

It can be scary for a number of reasons, one being strong, synthetic drugs like fentanyl. Sometimes a recurrence of use can be deadly as too many family members tragically know.

What is also tough about this is that we can help our loved one *with* change, but we can't *make* them change. We can celebrate with them and encourage them, but we cannot control the outcome.

So if it's likely that part of our loved one's recovery is a recurrence of use, what can we do as family members? How can we support them if or when they relapse?

As we shared earlier, one of the keys is information. Let's talk about what recurrence of use means and how we can support our loved ones with motivation for change when they experience it.

There are three different types of relapse, not just the physical act itself. Let's take a look at them and how we can support our loved ones at each stage.

Emotional Relapse

- Experiencing emotions and behaviors that can lead to relapse without actively thinking about using.
- Signs include isolation, skipping meetings, focusing on others' issues, obsessing about resentments, and poor sleep or nutrition.
- Family members and loved ones can help by modeling and encouraging healthy activities and self-care as well as encouraging connection with friends and supports in recovery. Recognizing they might be in an emotional relapse can help prevent further stages like mental relapse.

Mental Relapse

- Internal conflict between wanting to use and wanting to stay sober.
- Signs include cravings, reminiscing or glorifying past use or past using relationships, downplaying consequences, lying, bargaining, planning to use while staying in control, and seeking opportunities to relapse.
- Family members and loved ones can help their loved one recognize and avoid risky situations as well as understand that thoughts of using and cravings are normal. Acknowledging that thoughts and feelings are not facts can be helpful at this stage to help the person separate the thought or feeling with behavior. For example, just because they are having using thoughts does not mean they have to act on them. Bringing

these thoughts and feelings into the light can help not only affirm the person's feelings but also lessen their influence.

Physical Relapse

- Resuming substance use after a period of abstinence.
- Today researchers differentiate between a "lapse" (initial use) and a "relapse" (uncontrolled use), but this distinction might minimize the seriousness of a lapse. There is also important new language that suggests the use of the word "relapse" may be stigmatizing. Using the phrase "recurrence of use" may be helpful to avoid perpetuating stigma.
- Family members and loved ones can help by extending love with healthy boundaries. Recognizing the high-risk situations caused by a recurrence of use or multiple recurrences can lead loved ones to prepare with medications that can help, such as opioid overdose reversal medications or testing strips. Being prepared can help the family member feel ready to address a tough and disappointing situation.*

Understanding the different types can help us understand our loved ones and the truth that a recurrence of use can be a normal part of recovery.

It can be tough to think about a recurrence of use as a part of recovery. But the good news is that just because there is a recurrence of use does not mean that recovery is over. It does not mean that your loved one did something *to* you or to the family. It might be disappointing, but we can assure our loved ones that they are not a disappointment. They are loved. Letting them know that we understand that relapse can be a part of the journey can be the impetus for continued change.

---

* After a physical relapse, it is likely time for your loved one to revisit treatment options. Check out the back of this book for more resources and support.

Remember, "staying involved has the power to help your loved one change course."[5] Staying involved even when we might feel disappointed in our loved one's choices or actions or their rocky recovery journey has the power to support them along the way. But you don't have to do this alone. In community, together, we can trudge the road.

Charting a New Course

When I started my recovery journey as a teen, both my parents and I thought going away to "treatment" was like taking an antibiotic. Take one pill in the morning with food and by the end of the ten-day treatment, you will be cured.

I recall resisting this treatment as much as my smoky eyes and '90s grunge flannel could. I even went so far as to hide out on the back floor of my then boyfriend's Monte Carlo, driving around town listening to Limp Bizkit or early Eminem.

Treatment does not work that way, as we know today from the science and from experience. Just like many illnesses are becoming antibiotic resistant, treatment is not always a one-and-done approach to wellness. It is also no longer seen as the only way to begin or sustain lasting change. As we've been exploring and as you will see later (in the resources at the end of the book), there are many options for treatment and recovery support that can be individualized based on what we need.

We also know that part of the longevity of the journey (remember, it's a marathon, not a sprint) can be acknowledging that substance use may be just *one small part* of what needs healing, what needs change. Along with addressing substance use and misuse is a need for our loved ones to go deeper: to dig into root causes and address mental and physical health. As mentioned earlier, our loved ones also need to practice change. Change isn't a decision; it's a way of life.

I've developed the Practice Change Theory, which is one way to think about change and how to support a sustained recovery for our loved ones, even if recurrence of use is a part of what our family experiences together. The loop centers on these main areas:

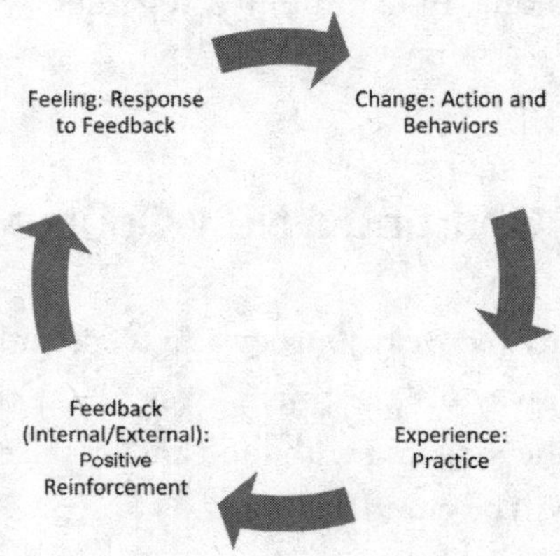

Practice Change Theory

This is how change can happen in the recovery process. It begins with an action of change (e.g., stopping opioid use or beginning therapy for depression and anxiety), moves to practicing this change (and giving your brain time to get used to the new behaviors), getting positive feedback and reinforcement from loved ones for new actions and behaviors, and having an emotional response to this reinforcement (e.g., increased self-confidence, feelings of value and worth).

If this is one way change happens, how can families and loved ones be involved in supporting it?

First, it is helpful to think about change in the context of our own lives. Whether our change is a diet, a habit, moving, or beginning a relationship, if you are breathing you've gone through a significant change at some point. Thinking back to some of the feelings associated with change can help us have empathy for our loved one's experience. Change can be hard *and* change can take time.

Consider these questions:

- What helped you feel ready to make a change?
- What motivated you to take action?
- How did it feel right before you were about to make a change? Were you excited? Anxious? Fearful? Ambivalent?
- Was the change sudden or gradual?
- Did the change go as planned or were there delays you didn't expect?
- Did you have support? If not, what was it like to go through the process alone? If yes, what was it like to have a support system?

• • • • •

When we love someone in recovery, we can recognize that change can be challenging.

• • • • •

Even if the specifics are different, we can come from a place of compassion and empathy. To be human is to struggle with change. To be human is to need others to understand what we are going through, to be seen and heard, and to be supported along the way.

Don't Look on the Bright Side

There is a toxicity in "bright-siding" that applies to this part of our conversation. I love this concept that was introduced to me by Stephanie Duncan Smith in her memoir *Even After Everything.*[6] As our loved ones are going through change, we don't have to sugarcoat the experience. It is tough. But we can still hang on to hope.

There is a difference between positivity and hope. We can be positive and hope for the best, and we can hope that our loved one will change. We can trust that they will continue in the loop or cycle of change. But we can also be realistic that the road might be bumpy. It might look different than we expected or wanted.

Remember, we *trudge* the road.

We don't have to bright-side our situation. We can confront it with realism *and* faith, tempered trust *and* hope. It might take time for our loved one to seek change. That's okay.

> People with substance problems respond with significantly less resistance to kindness and respectful treatment (as do the rest of us). So don't wait for your loved one to "hit bottom"—it can be dangerous, and problems are more treatable the sooner they are caught. And don't lose hope in the face of resistance from your loved one. Resistance is subject to change.[7]

As our loved one is practicing change, or perhaps just treading water, we can show up and choose to love first. We can show kindness and respect. We can ask for help from God or our people when it is hard.

On Waiting Well

Anyone who has tried to lose those pesky pounds knows how good it feels to have the jeans fit again. You know, the ones at the back of your closet that you are hanging on to because you hope that one day you might wake up and slip them on and get a side glance at your rear and smile.

Yes, the hard work has paid off.

Or maybe we donate those jeans because they don't fit and perhaps will never fit again. And that's okay too. Soft is good. Maybe we are tired of trying to fit into something old. Perhaps it feels good to be bursting at the seams, ready for something new, ready for change.

Anyone who has also struggled with a health condition like

cancer, heart disease, diabetes, hypertension, obesity, or substance use disorder knows that remission or recovery or wellness can look different in different seasons. It can shift and change like the shores of the Great Lakes (or like my pants' range of sizes).

Due to things like stigma, addiction is treated differently than other human conditions. But as loved ones, we can choose hope—not a sunny optimism that has blinders on but a steady support even when our loved one's recovery journey looks different than we want. Even if we are tired of the waiting.

During those times we might benefit from a common prayer shared during many recovery support meetings:

God grant me the serenity
to accept the things I cannot change;
courage to change the things I can;
and wisdom to know the difference.

Or the full version of the poem by Reinhold Niebuhr, which is less well known:

God, give us grace to accept with serenity
the things that cannot be changed,
Courage to change the things
which should be changed,
and the Wisdom to distinguish
the one from the other.
Living one day at a time,
Enjoying one moment at a time,
Accepting hardship as a pathway to peace,
Taking, as Jesus did,
This sinful world as it is,
Not as I would have it,
Trusting that You will make all things right,

If I surrender to Your will,
So that I may be reasonably happy in this life,
And supremely happy with You forever in the next.
Amen.[8]

Remember that the research provides a glimpse of hope on the horizon. No matter where you are on your journey or where your family member is, if everyone is still breathing, change is possible. The key is being "as willing to change as you want your loved one to be."[9]

Remember

Recovery is a process of change that often includes a recurrence of use. Change is not a moment in time but a way of life.

Reflect

- In what ways have you been misinformed about the nature of sustained recovery?
- How does this concept that "recovery is a process and not a destination" change your thinking of your loved one's experience?

Chapter 12

Recovery Revival

All great spirituality is about what
we do with our pain.
—Richard Rohr, *Adam's Return*

She walked into the fellowship hall and was surprised by the rainbow of balloons, sprinkle decor, and cupcakes. Her husband had arrived a little earlier, and now she knew that tonight's speaker meeting at the church was going to be different.

First Recovery, a growing recovery community in Oak Ridge, Tennessee, hosted a surprise baby party for Matt and Melinda Holder, leaders in the church and in the recovery community. They were expecting their second son any day.

At the party there was laughter, the wide eyes of newcomers unfamiliar with the fun of recovery (we are not a glum lot), and tears. The common range of emotions on Wednesday nights at this small town in the foothills of East Tennessee.

Instead of a traditional speaker, the community invited shares of gratitude. Popcorn-style proclamations of thanks peppered the fellowship hall. People spoke of gratitude for their second chances, for those who had impacted them, for the room they were gathered in that night. More than one person talked about the impact of First Recovery and how the reason they were there, the reason they were alive, was because of the support they received from people in the church.

Melinda Holder shared something that night that has stuck with me: "In recovery we find family."

It made me think about the fact that many of us do not come from healthy households. We don't learn how to love in a healthy way. Some of us grow up in supportive homes with all the trimmings, but we are bent on self-destruction. We don't feel like we belong. Or perhaps addiction runs through the branches of our family trees—generations of struggle with the bottle or other substances.

Psalm 68:6 says, "God sets the lonely in families, he leads out the prisoners with singing." It is one of my favorite passages of Scripture because so many of us find this to be true. When we feel the most alone, scared, tired, and ready for a new way to live, God shows up and brings people into our lives who support us and love us in the way we need.

In recovery we are welcomed into a new family.

With open arms we experience (sometimes for the first time) "you belong here; you are welcome here."

There are many churches that cause immense harm, aggravate trauma, and perpetuate stigma. But there are many recovery communities (inside and outside the church) where people find or rekindle their faith. Ministries like First Recovery remind us that there are faith-based spaces that do provide support. An open door, not a closed fist. A "welcome in" and not a "stay out."

Not only does this ministry provide meetings, housing scholarships, employment help, basic-needs assistance, food, and volunteer opportunities for the folks it serves, it was also a site of the Mobilize Recovery 2024 Bus Tour. On a warm and sunny fall day, national advocates and former *American Idol* winner Noah Thompson came to celebrate recovery and honor the faith-based recovery pathway that is shared within and outside its doors.

If you walk into First Recovery on a Wednesday night, you first walk by the Overdose Aid Kit (or OAK) in the hallway, which contains lifesaving opioid overdose reversal medication and fentanyl testing strips.

You will be welcomed by Judy near the coffee, who passes out sugary treats, gives welcoming hugs, and says "I love you" without reservation.

You will see Dan, a decades-long church member who admits that while he doesn't identify with being in recovery himself, he identifies with a community that is so loving and has such a strong sense of comradery. And Susan and Shawn, sitting in the pews along the wall, tearing up and nodding with compassion as stories are shared.

You will hear Heather's contagious laugh and see her bright eyes.

You will hear Matt's gentle welcome and prayer and perhaps notice baby Hinton smile at the folks sitting in the row behind him, bouncing on Melinda's knee.

You will see people from treatment programs and sober living houses and people from nearby towns who keep coming back because they have found connection.

If you show up on a Wednesday night you might find us celebrating a recovery milestone or a baby on the way. Or there may be honest sharing and conversation about the challenges of our journeys and the joys of recovery. No matter what we are up to on a given night in Oak Ridge, Tennessee, I can guarantee that you will find a place of true belonging and connection.

This experience isn't unique to Tennessee. There are recovery ministries and spaces around the world that exemplify the spiritual side of recovery.

You Follow Who?

Today Christianity (in some circles) is not associated with a way of being; it's attached to an agenda, one as polarizing as the arctic. Either you are in the camp or living outside of it. For those of us in recovery, our faith can be a point of contention too.

According to a Facebook post I shared, when I say the word *Christian*, what comes to mind for many is "judgmental," "hypocritical," and "toxic."

Words like *forgiving, loving, kind, encouraging, helpful, selfless* rarely make the cut. In some circles, at least.

I can feel the hurt in these simple words. And I've heard stories of incomprehensible harm being done by those who claim to be religious. Words can carry so much damage and, instead of freedom, spread captivity. Many of us in addiction recovery have experienced significant religious trauma and hurt—both in churches and in recovery communities.

Maybe as a family member or affected loved one, you have felt othered or disregarded by your faith family because of your loved one's substance use problems or even their misunderstood recovery. Maybe you've felt too ashamed to walk through those doors on Sunday. Maybe it is difficult to think that there is a spiritual side of recovery at all. Maybe you, like me, have been hesitant to be more bold about your faith in some recovery spaces.

This is why for many in recovery and our families, a spiritual path is a thorny one, despite many recovery programs having a deeply spiritual and religious history. It can be challenging to even bring up faith in some circles (and some circles of my dear friends). I get it. I've been there. I have a long and complicated history of faith and a spiritual side to my own recovery.

If this is you and this section is tough for you—or you think you know where this is going—I'd like to encourage you, invite you, to keep reading. You might be surprised where we end up together.

The Move of the Spirit

For those well-versed in AA literature, you may know the origin story of AA, a program that has helped millions of people since its birth on June 10, 1935. Its founders, Bill Wilson (Bill W.) and Dr. Robert Holbrook Smith (Dr. Bob), thought up the idea while Bill W. was hospitalized because of his alcoholism.

Bill W. was barely surviving the treacherous height of his addiction, lying in a hospital bed, desperate. He shared:

> All at once I found myself crying out, "If there is a God, let him show himself! I am ready to do anything!" Suddenly the room lit up with a great white light. I was caught up in an ecstasy which there are not words to describe. It seemed to me, in my mind's eye, that I was on a mountain and that a wind not of air but of spirit was blowing. And it burst upon me that I was a free man.[1]

For many of us, including one of the founders of an ongoing worldwide movement of recovery support, a spiritual experience, awakening, encounter, or conversion is the beginning of our lives as new creations in recovery.[2] As with Bill W. and the immediate lifting of his desire to drink, there is a miraculous turn of personality, behavior, and actions that can point to those around us, our loved ones, a change that feels almost otherworldly—or is.

What many might not know (including me before I read more about it), was that the founders of AA built the program that many of us know today four years after this experience in the hospital room. There were other influences to this program, including a deeply spiritual and Christian foundation.

One of the main influences to modern-day AA was the Oxford Group, originally from Great Britian. An episcopal clergyman named Samuel Moor Shoemaker Jr. also had a huge role in the spiritual components of the program. Bill W. and Dr. Bob attended meetings in New York with Shoemaker and blended lessons learned from the Oxford Group into a new model of support. Oxford Group ideals that centered on confession, character defects, making amends, and being of service made it into what we now call the 12 steps.[3]

From these beginnings a worldwide phenomenon was born, one that attracts religious, spiritual, agnostic, and atheist members alike.

But how? What is it about this traditionally religious program that is appealing to so many, including those who may have been burned by religion or those who reject it altogether?

Author and self-proclaimed stoic Ryan Holiday mentions recovery in his books because he is cool. I venture to guess that he also does this because the philosophy of recovery and the 12 steps include facets that transcend the wisdom of the ages, secular or not. He shares in one of his bestselling books, *Stillness Is the Key*:

> The step that many addicts—particularly the ones who fancy themselves thinkers—struggle with intensely is the acknowledgement of the existence of a higher power. They just don't want to admit that they "have come to believe a Power greater than themselves could restore them to sanity."[4]

And yet, surrender (not necessarily belief) is what first propels many of us to look upward and outward and toward something outside ourselves. This surrender goes beyond the confines of any steps of the recovery journey. It's bigger than how we (meaning humans) have organized the recovery experience.

There is a story about Ben, a surgeon in his mid-fifties who retired and quickly spiraled into active addiction using alcohol, pot, cocaine, and sex.[5] It was one of those spirals that people are surprised about. A doctor? In his fifties? Just the notion of a quick spiral for someone like Dr. Ben checks our own bias around addiction, doesn't it?

Dr. Ben goes on to share about a spiritual experience he had.

While buying crack, a stranger showed up and somehow encouraged him to go to treatment. He was desperate and tired of living, so he was ready to try anything.

While in treatment he was contemplating leaving. He had fifty bucks and no reason to stay. He didn't think there was another way to live. He said,

> All of a sudden a sense of peace came over me and I didn't see it, but I felt the presence of a person, and in my mind that person was Jesus. It was strange. I was sort of embarrassed. I felt his presence, and then a peace for no more than three or four minutes. This seemed to be part of a message. I was set to come in from the cold. And then I listened and let these people help me. I realized that it was not about judging, it was about acceptance.

From that point on Ben decided to stay and give sobriety a try. He was open and had a willingness to accept the help that was being offered to him after this spiritual experience. He said even years later he thinks back on this time. It is a "spiritual tool that continues to impact me. It gets richer and leaves me less depressed, less isolated, and less upset with what's wrong with me."[6]

There are similarities when we examine Bill W.'s and Ben's stories. And I've heard countless ones in meetings over the years. I've even had my own version of these stories—movements of spirit that are life-changing, illuminating. Following Jesus into a new pathway of recovery.

Has your loved one experienced the same? If so, how do you feel about it? Can you relate, or is it difficult to imagine this kind of spiritual experience or conversion?

For many people in recovery, faith is a part of our journey of healing. In some places in the world we can even say that a recovery revival is happening.

We Agnostics?

When I met with Dr. Asia Ashraf, I admittedly did not think about the time zone difference. I was just nibbling on lunch when I started the virtual meeting and quickly realized my Western ignorance on the issue of time zones.

"Good afternoon," I shared enthusiastically until I looked closer at the screen. It was dark, and Dr. Ashraf looked like it was not anywhere near workday hours.

"It's about ten o'clock where I am in Pakistan," she said.

Immediately I offered a flurry of apologies.

What came next in our conversation is something that still rocks me to my core.

Dr. Ashraf is a direct rehabilitation and consultant psychologist at Greenfield Hospital of Psychiatry in Pakistan. Her expertise extends to training professionals globally through organizations like the United Nations Office on Drugs and Crime and the Colombo Plan, an intergovernmental organization supporting developing nations with substance use prevention and myriad other things.

Because of its proximity to Afghanistan and the region's role as a transit corridor for drugs, substance use is a huge issue where she lives.

"Substance abuse is a huge pandemic in my country, and it is not a top priority of the government due to political issues," Dr. Ashraf said. The burden of tackling addiction largely falls on private organizations and international initiatives. As mentioned earlier, addiction is still viewed as a moral failing in many parts of Pakistan, adding to the stigma and making it harder for families to seek help.

Despite substance use recovery professionals like Dr. Ashraf, there are archaic approaches to treatment occurring in countries like Pakistan. "Unfortunately, maltreatment is common in Pakistan, with practices like cold turkey, confinement, and even beating still used in treatment facilities."[7] Such experiences make families fearful of seeking help and can lead to further trauma and resentment.

What is incredible is non-Western countries, while experiencing this level of trauma surrounding addiction treatment, are also experiencing revival. *Christianity Today* magazine published an article titled "Finding Sobriety—and Jesus—in Vietnam's Christian Drug Rehabs," recounting amazing happenings in treatment centers for men throughout Vietnam.

While I'd love for the word *rehab* to be replaced with non-stigmatizing language, national magazines like *CT* are highlighting a trend going on all over the world and on every continent. The spiritual wave happening is undeniable.

Wherever you fall on a spectrum (or non-spectrum) of faith or belief, it is tough to deny that spiritual experiences and conversions happen at significant rates for those of us in or seeking recovery. Spiritual well-being is connected to our sobriety and recovery journeys.

In Vietnam, leaders of their communist regime wonder why faith-based treatment centers in the country are helping people to stop using substances and change their lives.[8] In many areas, mandatory programs are known for human rights violations and abuses. The positive outcomes for this type of "treatment" are very low (if not nonexistent), and many people end up worse off than when they were forced to go.[9]

There is no trauma-informed care, only tactics that focus on punitive, archaic measures similar to the ones that Dr. Ashraf shared with me. In places like the Greenfield clinic, women like Dr. Ashraf are leading the charge to bring more humane treatment that opens opportunities for loved ones and family members to get well.

On the other hand, according to people like Nam Quoc Trung, the founder of the Aquila Center, a wave of new faith-based programs is changing public perception about what it means to be in recovery and how people can get there. Trung shares that "God chose those people who are already rejected by society, those people who are nothing in man's eyes, to reveal his glory. . . . Right now, my life is sweeter than any billionaire's life."[10]

Something is happening in treatment and recovery centers and services where evidence-based approaches are used and where the whole person is treated: body, mind, and soul.

Not all of us have dramatic spiritual conversions like Saul on the road to Damascus (Saul, a persecutor of the early church and Jesus followers, later became the apostle Paul), who was struck blind and thrown off his horse.

But I want to be clear: Some of us do.

Maybe not in the same fashion, but something unexplainable and mysterious can happen when we turn our lives over to the care of something—Someone.

The Spirituality Behind the 12 Steps

Thus far we have talked a bit about the history of AA and how it came to be as well as how it was rooted in a spiritual experience (or a series of them) with faith as its backbone. The steps, some believe, are central to not only recovery but a more faith-filled life.

I love what John Ortberg shares in his book *Steps: A Guide to Transforming Your Life When Willpower Isn't Enough*: "AA got the Twelve Steps from the church. And now the church needs them back. Actually, all humanity needs them."[11] For many, the 12 steps are a cornerstone of sorts—or lead to one.

The following chart outlines the key themes from an excellent resource called "The Twelve Steps and Their Biblical Comparisons."[12] You will see that each step has an underlying spiritual principle and key theme.

Many faith-based programs have built successful and evidence-based programs with this model as a foundation. Programs like Life

Recovery, Celebrate Recovery, Recovery Church, Re:generation, just to name a few, have been able to bring a spiritual foundation to the recovery process. Understanding the spiritual foundation of the 12 steps can help us to learn more about the spiritual experiences of those we love.

Before we dive into this, I want to say that not everyone finds recovery (or a deepened faith) through the 12 steps. While this is a helpful framework for many, it's not for everyone. There are also many who start recovery through the 12 steps and go on to live a healthy life outside of the program. Some find and maintain recovery without formally going through any step-based program.

In some circles this might be controversial to say, and I'm okay with that. I'm not including this section because I think it's the only way to stay sober. But it's one of the ways that your loved one may come to a deepened faith or strengthened recovery and a helpful framework for family members and loved ones to understand. The 12 steps are the foundation that many of the other recovery pathways, formal treatment programs, and peer support services are built on today (including the secular ones).

Here are the 12 steps and brief notes on how they connect to spiritual principles and themes.

Step 1

Step Statement: We admitted we were powerless over alcohol—that our lives had become unmanageable.

Spiritual Principle: Honesty & Surrender

Spiritual Theme: Admitting Powerlessness

Key Focus: Recognizing the inability to control addiction and surrendering self-sufficiency

Foundation Verse: "I know that good itself does not dwell in me, that is, in my sinful nature. For I have the desire to do what is good, but I cannot carry it out." (Romans 7:18)

Step 2

Step Statement: We came to believe that a Power greater than ourselves could restore us to sanity.

Spiritual Principle: Hope & Faith

Spiritual Theme: Belief in a Higher Power

Key Focus: Trusting that God can restore sanity and bring healing

Foundation Verse: "For it is God who works in you to will and to act in order to fulfill his good purpose." (Philippians 2:13)

Step 3

Step Statement: We made a decision to turn our will and our lives over to the care of God as we understood Him.

Spiritual Principle: Trust & Commitment

Spiritual Theme: Surrendering to God's Will

Key Focus: Making a decision to let God take control of one's life

Foundation Verse: "Therefore, I urge you, brothers and sisters, in view of God's mercy, to offer your bodies as a living sacrifice, holy and pleasing to God—this is your true and proper worship." (Romans 12:1)

Step 4

Step Statement: We made a searching and fearless moral inventory of ourselves.

Spiritual Principle: Courage & Self-Examination

Spiritual Theme: Personal Inventory

Key Focus: Honestly assessing past actions, fears, and resentments

Foundation Verse: "Let us examine our ways and test them, and let us return to the LORD." (Lamentations 3:40)

Step 5

Step Statement: We admitted to God, to ourselves, and to another human being the exact nature of our wrongs.

Spiritual Principle: Integrity & Confession

Spiritual Theme: Confessing to God & Others

Key Focus: Acknowledging wrongs to God, oneself, and a trusted person

Foundation Verse: "Therefore confess your sins to each other and pray for each other so that you may be healed." (James 5:16)

Step 6

Step Statement: We were entirely ready to have God remove all these defects of character.

Spiritual Principle: Willingness & Readiness

Spiritual Theme: Releasing Defects of Character

Key Focus: Becoming ready for God to remove character flaws

Foundation Verse: "Humble yourselves before the Lord, and he will lift you up." (James 4:10)

Step 7

Step Statement: We humbly asked Him to remove our shortcomings.

Spiritual Principle: Humility & Transformation

Spiritual Theme: Asking God for Change

Key Focus: Actively seeking God's help in overcoming shortcomings

Foundation Verse: "If we confess our sins, he is faithful and just and will forgive us our sins and purify us from all unrighteousness." (1 John 1:9)

Step 8

Step Statement: We made a list of all persons we had harmed and became willing to make amends to them all.

Spiritual Principle: Forgiveness & Accountability

Spiritual Theme: Making Amends in Spirit

Key Focus: Preparing to make amends by identifying those harmed

Foundation Verse: "Do to others as you would have them do to you." (Luke 6:31)

Step 9

Step Statement: We made direct amends to such people wherever possible, except when to do so would injure them or others.

Spiritual Principle: Restitution & Justice

Spiritual Theme: Direct Amends

Key Focus: Taking action to reconcile relationships and repair harm

Foundation Verse: "Therefore, if you are offering your gift at the altar and there remember that your brother or sister has something against you, leave your gift there in front of the altar. First go and be reconciled to them; then come and offer your gift." (Matthew 5:23–24)

Step 10

Step Statement: We continued to take personal inventory and when we were wrong promptly admitted it.

Spiritual Principle: Perseverance & Daily Renewal

Spiritual Theme: Continued Self-Examination

Key Focus: Maintaining spiritual awareness through regular reflection

Foundation Verse: "So, if you think you are standing firm, be careful that you don't fall!" (1 Corinthians 10:12)

Step 11

Step Statement: We sought through prayer and meditation to improve our conscious contact with God as we understood Him, praying only for knowledge of His will for us and the power to carry that out.

Spiritual Principle: Prayer & Meditation

Spiritual Theme: Seeking God's Will

Key Focus: Deepening connection with God through prayer and guidance

Foundation Verse: "Let the message of Christ dwell among you richly." (Colossians 3:16)

Step 12

Step Statement: Having had a spiritual awakening as the result of these steps, we tried to carry this message to alcoholics and to practice these principles in all our affairs.

Spiritual Principle: Service & Purpose

Spiritual Theme: Carrying the Message

Key Focus: Sharing recovery and helping others through faith and service

Foundation Verse: "Brothers and sisters, if someone is caught in a sin, you who live by the Spirit should restore that person gently. But watch yourselves, or you also may be tempted." (Galatians 6:1)

What does spiritual health or spiritual fitness look like in recovery? For some of us it means working within these steps; for others it is working outside them. There are many ways to get well. Some come to a deepened faith journey through these steps, but there is more to the story (I'm raising my hand here). For many of us, recovery is an ongoing process of spiritual formation and a growing relationship with God.

Though you or your loved one may have different beliefs or experiences, what is helpful to consider is that there is a spiritual side of our journey. The steps and their spiritual principles and themes support many of us in living a totally new, healthy, and transformed life.

John Ortberg wrote that perhaps we all "crave inspiration, profound feeling, freedom from anxiety and inadequacy, a sense of well-being that comes from connecting 'beyond.' Perhaps we are all 'wired for ecstasy.'"[13] Perhaps we can all benefit from the steps, spiritual principles, and solid foundations they are built upon.

• • • • •

When you love someone in recovery, you can discover that spiritual health is a part of the recovery journey for many.

• • • • •

Maybe your loved one has not communicated with you about a dramatic or spiritual conversion, but perhaps you can tell that they have changed and you would like to understand why. Maybe they are working the 12 steps or, as I've heard someone describe it, the "first step called Jesus Christ." Maybe your loved one is attending Celebrate Recovery religiously and healing from not just addiction but other hurts and hang-ups.

When you are living in recovery, you will know. When you've been moved "by the power of a great affection," it will be undeniable.[14]

The authors of *The Twelve Steps: A Spiritual Journey* call them "Milestones in Recovery." They are a litmus test to check one's spiritual temperature. This list can equally apply to people in or seeking recovery, family members, and other loved ones. Below is a paraphrase of this helpful list.

When we are "spiritually fit," as one of my first mentors said,

- We are at ease with other people, including those in positions of authority (e.g., police officers, parents)
- We carry a strong sense of self and identity
- We take constructive criticism as helpful counsel
- We are drawn to people who are emotionally healthy and available
- We take action to love and care for ourselves
- We can be bold and advocate for our own wants, needs, and desires
- We have faith and a sense of peace, even during tough times
- We love and are attracted to people who take care of themselves
- We can express our emotions using "I feel" statements and don't personalize others' feelings
- We gain new skills that help us meet goals (e.g., job skills, education, hobbies)
- We weigh the advantages and disadvantages of taking certain action
- We lean on God for support with increasing measure[15]

Do you notice that your loved one has picked up a new hobby and is smiling more? Is your son or daughter spending time with people who seem to be emotionally intelligent and healthy? Does your spouse have a newfound (and sometimes eerie) peace during chaotic times of crisis? Our loved one's actions and demeanor can communicate that things have, in fact, changed.

Spiritual health or fitness may look different, depending on where you or your loved one is on the journey. What is important to remember is that for many people in or seeking recovery, there is a spiritual path too.

As family members we can be open to listening and learning more about the spiritual experience or conversion experience our loved ones may have gone through (or are going through currently).

Recovery is not just about sobriety; discovering a newfound faith or rekindling past beliefs may be a part of the journey.

No matter how you feel about this chapter, maybe there is a common ground that we can all stand on. We can share a love of life and a hope in our loved ones.

Our loved ones might just discover or deepen their faith downstairs in a church basement where the coffee is cold and laughter has a pitch of joy. Maybe for some of us, we meet Jesus in upstairs spaces, in stained-glass sanctuaries. Maybe we are still unsure of the whole "God thing," but one thing we do know for sure: We feel welcomed and at home in recovery. We've finally found our people, a family.

Recovery is community in many ways. It can be a community of solid faith or unsure doubt or exploration. It is also where we can explore and find healing for those parts of us that have been hurt by religion.

Maybe *Christian* doesn't have to be a dirty word. Maybe it can be a freeing identity that brings life for people in or seeking recovery and our loved ones.[16] Maybe spiritual revival can bring light back to the eyes and recovery into our communities.

I like what Reverend Mark Flynn shared when I asked for his thoughts on faith and recovery:

> Any church which wants to support those in recovery or their family members needs to regularly and consistently challenge the comfortable mask we wear around one another suggesting "we are all doing really well." Almost all of us are struggling in life. To be a community which stops treating those whose issues and addictions become public as unusual, or out of the norm, is a great gift we can give to everyone, those in recovery and those who are not.[17]

Whether we personally identify with being in recovery or not, we can take off our masks and connect in a new community in honest and meaningful ways. Maybe we can, like the recovery community in Oak Ridge, Tennessee, welcome one another into a new family. We can encourage each other in both our recovery and in our spiritual formation. Because for many of us, the recovery journey involves a deepening faith.

Remember

Spirituality can be a central part of the recovery journey, although many have experienced religious hurt or trauma. Learning about our loved one's spiritual journey can help us to understand and support them.

Reflect

- How do you feel about the 12 steps and the principles behind them?
- Why do you think you feel this way?
- Are you willing to think about them differently? How?

Chapter 13

Navigating Resources and Promoting Change

We want to see more people
get the help they need.
—Jeremiah Calvino,
cofounder of Recovery.com

Her voice was trembling and the desperation was palpable: "She agreed to go to treatment today. I started making calls and . . . nothing. It's like a maze I can't find my way out of."

Or a loved one's cautious yet hopeful plea: "He is leaving treatment and doing amazing. But now he needs a safe place to go that has accountability and peer support. We aren't sure where to look for the right type of housing or what's next."

This is the experience of too many family members, behavioral health professionals, and advocates. When we are trying to support our loved ones along a recovery journey, what do we do? How can we help our loved ones find treatment and other resources? What kinds of support do they—and we—need? Do the options change over time?

I've spent countless hours on hold trying to find a recovery home bed or a spot in treatment for someone with or without insurance, with or without Medicaid. It can be a maddening and very tragic pursuit, especially when research shows that the window when someone is ready for change *and* ready for treatment can be brief. Each second is precious; each second on hold feels like an eternity of our loved ones slipping through our hands, slipping through the cracks again.

Bill Stauffer shares this:

> And the experience almost universally that I've heard from family members is that they thought they would have an experience similar to a medical system where they would reach out, contact somebody, and that there would be help available. And that these services would be supported and funded. Sadly, we don't have that. And so often it's a big runaround until they can access the kinds of things that are meaningfully helpful to them and their families.[1]

I've heard countless family members talk about the frustration of navigating a system that is complex and sometimes based on a "pay to play" model of support. If you have the funds to private pay for expensive, inpatient treatment programs, you can get in relatively quickly. If you are on government assistance with no or limited insurance coverage, sometimes the options are near zero.

For many families, navigating recovery resources is not only complicated but entirely new. When we are thinking expansively about recovery and that it is more than just "getting treatment," there are even more options to consider.

Thanks to Stauffer, other advocates and affected family members, and innovative businesses and organizations, things are changing. "What we're seeing is people who can help them navigate those processes, and they're also advocating for changing them so that we do have a service system that is more responsive to the needs of family."[2] This is good news: We don't have to navigate this alone, just like our loved ones don't have to navigate recovery alone. There are incredible resources (some I'll share about shortly) that want to help you find the support you or a loved one needs.

An important first step is understanding that when we say "treatment and recovery resources," we do not just mean inpatient treatment where your loved one packs a bag and goes to a building and stays there until the program is over. There are innumerable pathways that we can practice to support long-term, sustained wellness and—for many of us—reduced or abstained substance use. Different levels of care provide support dependent on the stage of recovery or need.[3]

"Rehab" (the stigmatizing way to refer to addiction treatment) is not the only starting point for change,[4] although for many (I'm raising my hand) it's an important point along the road to sustained recovery and increased quality of life. The good news is that our loved ones can begin right where they are (and we can too).

My friend and colleague Tom Farley, brother to the late actor and comedian Chris Farley and person in long-term recovery, works for an amazing company called Recovery.com. He shares that it is imperative for families to have a clear path for supporting their loved one. It was something that he wished he had for his brother and even for himself as he explored treatment for his own substance use disorder.

> Anyone in recovery will tell you how critical connection is to their healing. Yet most will also share that a feeling of isolation can dominate the early stages of the healing journey. That was true for me, and I'm certain it was true for my brother, Chris.

Recovery.com was created in 2017 as an unbiased source for finding a pathway to healing through different addiction and mental health treatment options. Tom goes on to share:

> Recovery.com not only helps people find the right treatment options but starts to build in connection from the very start.

> Individuals and families can search for resources that answer their questions, and they can hear stories from people at all stages of recovery. These are the things that help everyone overcome fear and break down stigmas, which then pave the way for connection. While I wish such a resource had existed for Chris, our parents, and me, today I get to see that Recovery.com is helping so many others find recovery. For me, that is so encouraging.[5]

Recovery.com includes tens of thousands of treatment and recovery support service providers around the world and shares direct access to points of contact at treatment centers. It's super simple for families and loved ones to use. You can search for treatment centers that fit your needs based on location, insurance coverage, specialty treatment, and more. Then you can compare programs side by side and connect directly to a resource to begin your own recovery journey. It's more than a directory of available treatment—it's a lifeline. Anyone, anywhere, can find the help they need.

Recovery.com is also a trusted resource online for addiction and related mental health content, including articles, videos, podcasts, and more. Not only do many of my friends work for and contribute to their efforts, I am also a partner in their content creation, writing, and editing. My coworkers here have the biggest hearts of any place I've worked.

I share about this incredible resource here because I believe in the mission of the company and have witnessed firsthand the real help it provides families in or seeking recovery. I've also felt in the past, as I've mentioned, the deep frustration of not knowing where to start or what to do when looking for help.

For those of us who have experienced similar confusion or frustration, or for those who have even given up because of an overwhelmed sense that *we are not getting anywhere* with all the calls, emails, and Google searching, keep reading.

Motivation and Change

What if you are frustrated not with navigating resources or finding treatment but with your loved one's seeming lack of motivation or resistance to change?

I love what author and recovery guide Richard Rohr shares: "Most of us were taught that God would love us if and when we change. In fact, God loves you so that you can change. What empowers change, what makes you desirous of change is the experience of love. It is that inherent experience of love that becomes the engine of change."[6]

I have heard countless people talk about the transformative power that someone else's belief in them and for them has had in their life. I have experienced this too. People believing in my own life change before I knew it was possible. It is as if their belief in me became my own, became a driving force for change.

Human relationships impact motivation. How we engage with, encourage, and support our loved one does make a difference, whether on the outset they appear "ready" or not. Because motivation can change; it is a "moving target."[7]

> Until recently, traditional methods of treatment for substance problems conceived of motivation as a fixed trait: you have it or you don't. People who supposedly didn't have the motivation to change were told to come back when they were "ready." Family members were coached to disengage, as there was nothing they could do until their loved one was "ready." Unfortunately (and sometimes tragically), this view left clinicians and family members on one of two sides, neither of which was helpful: they could passively wait for motivation to happen, or they could aggressively demand change.[8]

What helps or hinders motivation?

What leads us toward change is not some threshold or thing you cross into like a state line ("Now we are in Kentucky!"). It can be a gradual shift like the way the fog of the mountains appears at dawn, then fades into the forest. Here are several things that research shows can help support motivation.

What Helps Motivation

- Feeling understood and accepted
- Having a sense of agency and choices
- Having a clear "why" or sense of purpose
- Getting positive reinforcement and praise
- Seeing positive results (even if they may seem small at first)

What Hinders Motivation

- Feeling judged or misunderstood
- Having a sense of feeling forced or coerced
- Not having a clear "why" or reason for change
- Not having other options
- Getting negative feedback

How do people change? "Over time. With stops and starts, along a crooked line. With practice. With ambivalence . . . . When the trade-offs seem worth it. With a little help—sometimes a lot of help—from friends and family. With anguish. With effort. With joy."[9]

There are also stages of change that some evidence-based models promote. I've included helpful information about these and motivational interviewing in the back of the book (along with more great communication techniques). Communicating in a way that research shows helps (and does not harm) our loved ones is key to supporting and understanding recovery. It is helpful not just for encouraging our loved one to get help if they are struggling but to continue supporting their recovery into the future.

Here is a brief chart that outlines the concept as it relates to our loved ones along a recovery continuum and how we can support them in practical ways.

Stage of Change	Person In or Seeking Recovery	Where Loved One May Be	How a Loved One Can Support
Precontemplation	Doesn't see their substance use as a problem; may be defensive if confronted.	Frustrated, feeling helpless, or in denial about the severity of their loved one's addiction.	Avoid pushing too hard; express concern with love and nonjudgmental conversations. Educate yourself on addiction.
Contemplation / Getting Ready	Begins to acknowledge the problem but feels unsure or ambivalent about change.	Hopeful but unsure how to help; may feel caught between encouraging and pressuring change.	Listen empathetically. Offer support without pressure. Provide information on treatment options if they are open to it.
Preparation/ Readiness	Commits to making a change; may start exploring treatment options or support groups.	More involved, researching resources, setting boundaries, and offering practical support.	Help them find and access recovery resources (e.g., therapy, recovery meetings). Set clear but loving boundaries.
Action	Actively taking steps to recover (e.g., attending therapy, engaging in recovery programs, avoiding triggers).	Actively supporting recovery, possibly attending family support groups (e.g., Al-Anon).	Celebrate progress, encourage accountability, and maintain open communication.

Maintenance	Maintains sobriety, builds a new lifestyle, and handles relapses or setbacks constructively.	Encouraging continued growth, helping prevent relapse, and supporting long-term wellness.	Continue providing emotional support, encouraging healthy habits, and addressing any challenges together.

This chart emphasizes a process and can help us understand where our loved ones may be along their recovery journey. Recovery is, after all, a *process of change.*

Change also includes failure, missing the mark, setbacks, and obstacles. It is not a linear path; just like anything else worthwhile in life, it takes effort, sweat, and reflection. If your loved one seems to take one step forward and ten back, this doesn't mean their recovery isn't working. It's just taking time. And that's okay. It's normal.

When we fail or have failures (the Latin root of *failure* is "to disappoint") it often leads to fear that we will disappoint the people closest to us. You may have heard this from your loved one if they have a setback or difficulty telling you that they are struggling: "I just didn't want to disappoint you."

We don't want to fail. We don't want to let our family members or ourselves down. But understanding that this can be a part of the process is key to a broader picture of what recovery is. It is not a perfect road without bumps in the path. Indeed, there can be ruts or almost insurmountable summits. But the good news is that we have tools for supporting our loved one and navigating and understanding the available resources for each stage.

Navigating Recovery Together

Let's turn now to a practical section where we will walk through insights and tools for the journey. No matter where your loved one is, you can use this information like stepping stones when supporting them or navigating options—and supporting yourself in the process.

Recovery exists on a continuum, and it's not a linear one (perhaps I'm sounding like a broken record, but this is a point worth repeating). The more we are armed with information, the more we can fully support our loved ones. Instead of feeling like you are trapped in a maze, we can navigate recovery together.

Tool 1: Psychoeducation

Not to be confused with psychobabble (to all my therapist friends, I love you), psychoeducation is an integral part of the journey, whether during your loved one's struggle with substance use or along a recovery pathway. It is an excellent place to start.

While it is tough to admit we might not have all the answers and need to learn more about addiction recovery, education will help tremendously. Even if you are starting from a place of having a tremendous amount of knowledge, which you likely do, we can agree that there is always more to learn. You have already encountered psychoeducation in some earlier chapters (and perhaps you didn't even know it!).

Understanding can open important doorways to needed information. It also enables us to have compassion for our loved one's journey and patience when their choices or behavior might be confusing or even scary for us. This step in the process may be a beginning point, but as we like to say in recovery, "more shall be revealed" as we continue in our own healing as family members.

Examples of psychoeducation may include

- Books like this
- Resources and information from a therapist, counselor, recovery coach, or family recovery peer support provider
- Informational resources that describe symptoms, treatment, or recovery options
- Classes, workshops, virtual discussions, and other means for communicating information

Tool 2: Intervention

When you hear this word, you may (like me) have visions of an old show with washed-up celebrities who are lured into luxury rehabs lined with palm trees. I'd like to challenge us to broaden our view and think about intervention in a new way. While intervention can be the more traditional view of the concept (e.g., bring in a trained interventionist and have a family meeting where you lovingly confront your loved one), it can also happen in other ways.* At its core, it's about stepping in to help, an invitation to change.

Examples of what an intervention might look like in your family or with your loved one include

- Meeting with a trained counselor and interventionist who helps a loved one see the impact of their addiction and accept treatment.
- Another family member, close friend, or recovery coach having a one-on-one conversation using specialized communication skills (e.g., motivational interviewing) to encourage a struggling individual to seek therapy, outside support, or treatment.
- Meeting with a faith community or other community-based organization that supports addiction recovery.

---

* This next step may or may not be a stepping stone along your path of family recovery, and that's okay. It is listed here as a reference point or a possible option for support.

- A friend asking you to coffee and sharing that they are concerned, asking, "Is there anything I can do?" or "Are you okay?"
- A family therapy session or during family day at inpatient treatment when a counselor suggests that it might be time to think about getting support for the entire "family system" and not just your loved one struggling with substance use disorder.

Intervention types are varied and ultimately support a movement toward change.

Families can be trained in effective intervention strategies and communication techniques (more on this in a minute). Affected family members can also partner with interventionists who specialize in working with families. This is just one more tool for supporting our loved ones—and ourselves.

Tool 3: Peer Support

We all need support. When we have a loved one who is in or seeking recovery from addiction, it is imperative to have people in our life who we trust and who can speak to us from a place of empathy and shared experience. As we shared earlier, peer support is support offered by peers or people with shared lived experience. Often the people we trust are those who have been through similar experiences and who have come out on the other side of them.

When I surveyed affected family members around the world with Dr. Best, one of the key areas identified as being of the most help was peer support, which could include

- Family support groups like Al-Anon or other mutual aid groups that include individuals with shared lived experience.
- Faith-based recovery groups that promote holistic recovery, like Celebrate Recovery, and that may have an affected family member–specific group.

- One-on-one recovery coaching from people, including affected family members, who are trained and even credentialed in providing peer support. Reaching out to your local community-based recovery organization or health department may be a great first step in locating this type of support.
- Virtual peer support through various groups and organizations (see the list of resources at the back of the book).
- Informational peer support with other family members and friends who may provide an objective viewpoint, listen, and share empathetically.

Tool 4: Communication

Sometimes when talking to our loved one who is in or seeking recovery (or who is still in active addiction) it can feel like you are speaking two different languages. You may be wondering, *Will they ever understand where I am coming from? Will they ever see things from my perspective?*

How do we communicate with our loved ones in a way that propels them forward (and does not cause greater division and strife)? And also protects our own mental health? Does the way we communicate matter? How much weight or responsibility should we place on ourselves when it comes to this? After all, sometimes it does not matter what we say—their behaviors and substance use or even their recovery may not improve or change.

The important thing to keep in mind about communication is that it involves an exchange of information between the speaker and the listener. What we must consider as affected family members and loved ones is the state of our own hearts and minds—what *we* can control.

I have this bad habit of sometimes not pausing long enough to communicate after I'm irritated by an email, a snarky social media comment, or my husband. I also recall that in active addiction my filter was almost nonexistent. Screaming matches with my parents and friends were commonplace. It was as if we could not hear or understand each other—and what made matters worse is that my shouting drowned out any chance of hearing each other.

When it comes to communicating with our loved one, we can keep these things in mind:

- Have compassion.
- Practice active listening.
- Suspend disbelief and judgment.
- Use non-stigmatizing language.
- Focus on gratitude.

It's true. Have you ever been in a recovery meeting? If so, you have likely heard some of the most horrific stories and life experiences, and you have also likely heard some of the most amazing songs of praise. A room full of "eyes like sunshine" like my kids say. A room full of gratitude and hope.

One of the ways that I have worked on my own communication with loved ones who are struggling with addiction or in recovery is to practice active listening with a gratitude mind-set. I challenge myself to be quiet, still, and not focus on what counsel I can give or how I can help. I listen, and if the story is tough or challenging, I say just that: "This sounds so tough" or "What a challenging situation." I do not try to offer suggestions or solutions. I am just there. Afterward, I recenter my own thoughts and emotions by focusing on gratitude and sometimes by writing a gratitude list.

You are the expert in your own life. You likely know of other communication tools that are helpful for expressing yourself, setting boundaries, and staying motivated to continue walking alongside your loved one. I'd like to encourage you here to keep practicing what works. Keep the lines of communication open. Even when it's tough. Find the simple things to be grateful for. And if it ever feels impossible to have a conversation with your loved one, reach out for support.

Take a minute to brainstorm ways that you can practice these communication techniques. For each of the points, think of three ways you can practice these in conversation with your loved one.

- How can I have compassion?
- How can I practice active listening?
- How can I suspend disbelief and judgment?
- How can I use non-stigmatizing language?
- How can I focus on gratitude?

Tool 5: Recovery Pathways

We have already talked about recovery pathways and the importance of understanding that recovery is an expansive concept. It exists far beyond our traditional notions of what sobriety or "getting better" means.

Different pathways of recovery can include traditional intervention approaches, harm reduction, treatment (e.g., inpatient, partial hospitalization, and outpatient), recovery support services (e.g., recovery coaching, recovery housing, and vocational support), and sustained recovery approaches (e.g., volunteerism, vocation, education, and relationship skills).

We can recognize that there are diverse pathways to healing. No longer are we confined to only traditional models of treatment like those found in church basements. We can explore programs that aren't based on the 12 steps. We can integrate faith-based principles into traditional programs. We can take a chance and schedule a one-on-one meeting with a recovery coach with lived experience. We can, as affected family members, try a virtual meeting with other family members that is facilitated by someone with lived experience.

We can commit to learning more about the wide range of

recovery pathways. We can encourage our loved one by supporting an individualized instead of cookie-cutter approach. We can learn from other family members who have loved ones on different pathways and open our minds to new approaches that might feel scary until we have more information. Most importantly, we can walk alongside our loved one on whatever pathway they start or continue.*

Tool 6: Family Recovery Planning

Last is the concept of family recovery planning. This is like creating a road map, structure, or guide. I've created a free resource you can access through the URL in the Resources for Families at the back of this book.

A formal family recovery plan will help you examine priorities, set goals, and brainstorm ways—*with your loved one*—on how to understand and support them. It can act as a guide and as a reference for accountability and measuring progress, along with establishing communication strategies that support motivation and promote change.

Family recovery plans can also outline communication strategies, peer support, boundary setting, and other helpful resources for moving forward. It can be a formal printed-off PDF that everyone in the family signs or it can be an informal agreement sketched on a white board.

Elements of the family recovery plan include

- **Healthy boundary setting:** Boundaries are helpful ways to set up loving lines in the sand. I shared at the beginning of the book that my dad bought me groceries and took me out to eat when I was using. This loving action was helpful (giving me cash would not have been). Maybe a boundary for loved ones in

* In the appendix there is a detailed list of different types of recovery pathways.

recovery is to check in once a week for updates instead of texting them every hour to check in or make sure they are sober.

- **Recurrence-of-use plan:** Similar to the old-school "relapse prevention plan," this guide provides an agreed-upon outline for the person in or seeking recovery and their family. It isn't meant to convey distrust or unbelief of recovery, but it serves as an accountability point. For example, this could include something like, "If you have a recurrence of use, you will seek additional support like counseling or outpatient treatment if you'd like to continue living at home rent-free."
- **Recovery support strategies:** This can be a place to outline recovery pathways and indicate current pathways, past actions (and their results), and goals for future recovery supports. For example, maybe your loved one is in recovery housing and their goal is to transition to their own apartment next year with a sober roommate.
- **Sustained recovery:** Long-term recovery is amazing and requires different supports and understanding. For example, my husband knows that for me, exercise or movement is very important for my mental health. So is having time every week to volunteer or give back to the recovery community. Making sure you understand your loved one's nonnegotiables that help them sustain recovery is key. One of the biggest mistakes we can make is thinking that as the years go on, we are *good*. In fact, it is even more important to continue with what works. Just because we have been able to celebrate recovery milestones does not mean that we can stop doing what's helped us get to this point.
- **Personal Supports:** This may be one of the most important parts of family recovery planning. This is a place to reflect on those things that fill your cup. Maybe that is therapy, maybe that is training for a race, maybe that is having brunch with your friends. Make sure that you have a long list of personal

supports, activities, and encouraging relationships in your own life too.

Ultimately, family recovery planning will help to outline coping strategies and healthy actions while being a point of reference for your family. This structured plan also has templates for setting boundaries and recurrence-of-use plans, and it will encourage your long-term commitment to recovery as a family.

Navigating resources and promoting change is about so much more than getting our loved one into addiction treatment, although this is often an important step along the path. There are countless ways that we can support our loved ones, no matter what stage of the recovery continuum or stage of change they are on. Ultimately, supporting our loved ones is about showing up, using tools, and learning what works for our families together.

Remember

Navigating resources and promoting change can be extremely challenging for families. But there are tools we can use and knowledge we can gain that will help us think holistically about understanding and supporting our loved ones.

Reflect

- What tool or insight most applies or resonates with you?
- How have you been spurred to action or how has your thinking about supporting your loved one changed after reading this chapter?

PART 5

recovery is service

Chapter 14

Purpose Driven

Help others rise by sharing your unique gifts to make their lives better. By lifting others, you also lift yourself.
—Scott Strode

Christina looks like the kind of woman who might either give you a bear hug, send you home with a plate of leftovers, or take you Christmas caroling with her church choir. Yet there is a fierceness about her that I love. She appears gentle and kind, yet behind the approachableness is an intimidating momma-bear vibe.

When I learned more about her story, I was even more intrigued.

Christina grew up in a conservative church as a homeschooled kid without knowledge of the addiction crisis that plagued her hometown in Mississippi. Later, when she became a mom, she and her husband chose to homeschool their kids too—an intentionally chosen "bubble" because the world was nowhere Christina wanted to raise her children. She preferred overseeing the education of her children in the comfort and stability of her home just like she experienced.

Enter foster parent status. Christina's and her family's eyes were soon opened to the reality of addiction, and the bubble burst. This changed everything.

Christina shares in her award-winning memoir, *Curious*, that "our painful experiences may not leave wounds on our skin, but they always leave wounds on our souls. Sometimes the invisible wounds hurt the most and linger the longest."[1]

She did not know the pain of addiction, but she knew the pain of losing both parents while still a teenager: her mother to stage-three ovarian cancer and her father to lung cancer. By age twenty-four Christina knew what it felt like to be untethered without the anchor of family. That may be why her heart was moved by children who needed a home.

She and her husband became foster parents and started leading a foster care ministry at her church. One day a call came that was a turning point for her family and her life's purpose. Looking back, she recognizes it now, though at the time it felt overwhelming to agree. But she and her husband knew it was God's call on their life to open their home to a newborn baby.

> Within the hour we agree to take the baby. His name is Beckham, and this 5-pound 9-ounce treasure arrives on our doorstep a few hours later. I don't realize it yet, but this phone call just fused my life with the life of this mother—a woman who will open another new world to me, reshape my heart, and change my mind.[2]

Beckham's mother, Joanne, taught Christina that addiction isn't a choice and does not discriminate. Addiction has no skin color or language preference. No gender or age. And if our loved ones struggle, it doesn't mean that we have failed. It also doesn't mean that our kids or spouses or friends are "bad" or "dirty" or not worthy of our love, hope, and trust.

> Learning about what causes addiction hasn't made me less worried that my own kids might struggle. If anything, it has helped me see just how easily it can develop because of how broken and painful our world is. It doesn't mean our parenting failed, and it doesn't

> mean our kids are terrible. It's an indication that the hurt of a fallen world in all its array has found a place to set up camp in their hearts.[3]

Christina goes on to share that "maybe the best way we can help our kids is by having honest conversations with them about drugs, teaching them healthy coping skills for the pain in their lives, and modeling how to seek professional help when it's needed."[4]

Today Beckham lives with his mom, who is thriving in recovery. Christina includes a picture of them in her book, Joanne beaming and holding her son tight on her lap with the assurance of a woman who knows she is loved. Love is overflowing, and her son has the same look. The light in their eyes is evident.

Christina has since founded and now runs a nonprofit organization in Mississippi called *End It for Good*, dedicated to educating the community about the reality of addiction and the truth that punitive approaches to drug use won't work. The organization focuses on health-centered approaches for all people and families and a recovery-oriented philosophy of change and avenue for social policy reform.

Christina, and so many recovery advocates and affected family members like her, remind me of this gem of a quote by Timothy Willard, the author of *The Beauty Chasers*: "A kind of holy magic is enfolded into our daily acts of calling. By aiming to serve our neighbors with our gifts, abilities, and resources, we overlay society with what I like to call heaven culture."[5]

Purpose Is Proven

In early sobriety I needed something outside of myself to focus on. I needed a *why* that wasn't me. The same is true today. When we have a purpose outside of ourselves, "change becomes worth it."[6]

In the realm of addiction recovery, having a sense of purpose is significant. It enables us to face feelings of emptiness and hopelessness head-on. For many in 12-step fellowships like Celebrate Recovery or AA, the twelfth step comes to mind. We are to "carry the message" of recovery to others who are struggling. It is through being of service that we bring the transformative power of empathy and compassion—an unconditional acceptance.

The research today shows that not only does living with purpose and on purpose help us feel good, it is part of a thriving life. People who volunteer and give back, on average, live healthier and longer lives.[7] Some are even calling for more research in this area to promote volunteerism and giving back as a public health approach.[8]

When we discover meaning and new passions, we build a solid foundation for enduring sobriety. As family members, like Christina, we can also find purpose too. We can build toward a healthier life ourselves and for those around us. Purpose can look different for different people. Maybe it's volunteering at a meeting, maybe it's being a sponsor, maybe it's writing or speaking or going back to school or starting a family. Maybe it's opening your home to a child impacted by addiction.

It's okay to need more for our lives than sobriety for its own sake. If we are sober or in recovery for the sole purpose of abstaining from drugs and alcohol or mitigating harm, what will keep us motivated? What will keep us grounded in this path that has its mountains, true, yet also brings with it challenging valleys and sometimes unforgiving summits?

What We Can Learn About Purpose

These days I learn most from and look up to women in recovery who have been there. Susan Packard is one of these women whom I met while doing outreach for the Association for Recovery in Higher Education, a nonprofit that supports collegiate recovery.

Susan posted about a speaking engagement on Instagram and said,

> My friends sometimes ask why I still do this—get on airplanes and speak to large and small groups. . . .
>
> Here are three reasons, fresh from speaking at the Women's Summit Event at @BryantUniversity:
>
> Reason One: After the event, a high school student reached out to me on LinkedIn, promised me she would stay in touch, and follow her dreams.
>
> Reason Two: A woman mid-career told me that she's four years sober. I speak openly about being sober when I talk about emotional fitness, as recovery is one of its gold-star practices. How incredibly gratifying to hear that!
>
> Reason Three: A flash of someone running up as I was leaving the room and entrusting me with a magazine she is starting up. "You spoke of being brave. This is me being brave! . . ."
>
> To me, it's a privilege to show up for women coming after me. We embody for them ways to live their fullest, happiest, most artfully accomplished lives.

Susan's inspiring post stirred in me the notion that purpose can not only drive us but also help us to define our reasons for showing up and being present for others.

Don't Give Up

Without purpose we may wonder, *What's the point?*

Walk into any long-term care or nursing facility and you might feel a palpable sense of longing. Before centering my life on recovery, when I was still a young pup trying to find my way, I used to work with older adults. I can look back and know God was doing mighty things in my heart. He softened it and helped me to see life through the wisdom of the folks I was caring for. I didn't know at the time, but this service gave me a sense of purpose.

I heard repeatedly from older adults that they lacked purpose, especially those who struggled with depression and loneliness. They didn't understand what they were there for anymore after age had taken loved ones, mobility, homes, and more. Stripped from what much of the world says gives us that purpose—youth and possessions and physical strength—sometimes there was a shared sentiment that there was nothing left to live for.

You might sense the same walking through the halls of an inpatient treatment facility or a prison. A person without purpose is often a person without hope, and I'm not sure there is a sadder thing in the world. That's one of the reasons I'm a huge proponent of community building and mentorship, because I've seen and experienced firsthand the destructive power of a life without purpose. Of course, the older adults I worked with did have lives of purpose, even if they did not recognize it. Part of my job was helping them experience a *reason why* again.

Your family member may be thinking of going back to school to become a therapist, open a recovery home, or even write a book. Don't be surprised at this sudden need to be involved. It's important to foster ways to give back, as purpose is an integral part of the recovery journey.

We can be involved in encouraging activity and purpose for one another. Here are several ways you can support your loved one in finding purpose in their life and recovery or support their new purpose:

- **Encourage giving back or volunteering:** Volunteering can provide a renewed sense of purpose. You can encourage your loved one to get involved in a wide range of community service or other types of volunteer work, whether at your church, through a recovery organization or ministry, or other ways. These can be powerful experiences that show there is life after struggle with addiction.

- **Support educational pursuits:** Learning new ways to be of service and new skills can be life-giving and lead to a new sense of purpose. Whether it's going back to school and enrolling in a course, attending conferences and continuing education opportunities, or even just learning a new hobby like a musical instrument, art, or writing, supporting your loved one's new educational pursuits can be life-affirming and give encouragement for them to keep going.
- **Encourage setting personal goals:** Encouraging your loved one to set and pursue personal goals can help them stay motivated and cultivate meaning. Goals may feel overwhelming, or even scary, if they have had trouble following through or finishing in the past. But goals don't have to be excruciating; they can be fun and even holistic: running a race, reading a set number of books each month (one of my personal favorites), learning a new hobby. Having a target to aim toward can be helpful, and the confidence built when goals are accomplished is invaluable.
- **Celebrate simple wins and progress:** Recognize and celebrate achievements, no matter how seemingly insignificant. I have heard lots of friends talk about how even the act of getting up, getting ready, and making a bed can feel like a winning day compared to the hell of a day starting in active addiction. Finding even the simple things to praise and celebrate can help our loved ones shift to a progress and purpose-driven mind-set.
- **Foster healthy relationships:** A supportive network of friends and mentors who share your loved one's values can help foster a sense of shared purpose. Positive, healthy relationships provide emotional support and accountability. It can also be fun

to meet other like-minded and service-oriented people along the way!

Maybe as you are reading this you're feeling a bit discouraged because you wish your loved one had the motivation to want to go back to school, volunteer, or do anything besides stare at their cell phone screen or puff on their vape pen on your back deck. If this is the case, you're not alone. It can take time for those of us in recovery—or anyone—to lean into a new sense of purpose, to take a risk or try something new, to step outside our comfort zone and our own ego to be there for someone else, to truly believe that our lives have value and purpose.

When I said yes and started volunteering at the outpatient treatment center as a mentor, I had a new reason to show up in my own life and in early sobriety. Alex and Jon and Hannah and Amanda and all the other young people who listened when I shared my story (and I held back tears as they shared theirs) gave me a reason outside myself to keep going. In working with them, I came to believe that the struggle of my past life in active addiction and all the trauma I had been through could be redeemed. My addiction had a purpose. I could be a part of healing someone else's story.

• • • • •

When you love someone in recovery, remember that purpose is central to living a life of sustained recovery.

• • • • •

The pain has purpose. This took time to fully plant in my heart and take root. And of course, purpose can change with the seasons. But it is a driving force of recovery that supports long-term wellness.

It's why Susan Packard shares her story of recovery and rising in the ranks of business leadership to help other young women and college students. It's why Bill Stauffer started and now leads an organization helping thousands of people in Pennsylvania. It's why Christina Dent opened her home to a child impacted by addiction and was moved to be an advocate for addiction policy reform. It's why those of us in recovery are showing up in innumerable ways to be of service and not only help others but, in the process, help ourselves. It's why you might be doing the work you're doing in your own local community or even in your own home.

Purpose can be a slow burn. But once the fire is lit, it is amazing. Once your family member finds their purpose in recovery, everything changes. It's like staring out over the Grand Canyon: The beauty of it all might not make sense, but it's there and you can't unsee it even if you tried.

We are created on purpose for a purpose, yet addiction often steals this truth from us. We start to believe that we could just disappear—it doesn't matter, nothing matters—and that we are the furthest thing from lovable. We often believe that we have nothing to give. Our actions and the consequences of our substance misuse and addiction only solidify these claims, these lies. Not to mention what substance use does to our brain and thinking.

That's why any conversation about supporting loved ones through addiction and into recovery must start with helping our loved ones understand and cling to their true identities as beloved human beings with a reason for being.

Our Lives Make Ripples

Camping always seems like a good idea until we are actually there and not sleeping, cold, and dirty. My son always wants to throw stones into the water. Creeks, ponds, lakes—it doesn't matter; he wants to watch as heaviness drops into the glistening pool or the rushing mountain stream. He likes to follow the splash of the rock and how it disappears out of sight. He asks me to help him find flat stones that he brushes with the top of his gloved hand in the early fall morning. One, two, three, the flat stones dance on top of the water until they find their home in the mud.

It reminds me that we can make ripples.

When I had about four months sober, I wandered into the outpatient treatment center I've shared about because a young woman I met at a meeting had asked me to go with her. At the time I didn't think about insurance or referrals or that I probably needed to be a patient at this treatment center. I just went with her on a Tuesday evening to "group."

I'd been to inpatient treatment enough times to know that *group* meant uncomfortably sitting in a circle of chairs with strangers who share a bend toward problematic substance use and self-destruction. I said yes to my new friend because her eyes were wide, her voice was pleading, and I knew her fear:

Sobriety early on can be intimidating and scary.

My prediction was correct: It was uncomfortable. At first.

We sat down and immediately the group leader, Shelly, a counselor who I would come to know intimately, asked, "Who are you?"

I explained the situation, that I'd met my friend at a meeting and she asked me to come. Immediately Shelly asked how much time I had in recovery and I told her proudly, "Four months." I heard audible gasps. Four months felt like an impossible eternity to some. It did to me too.

Shelly was quiet for a moment. I could feel her looking into my eyes, searching them. Then she said, "We are looking for mentors. People with more than ninety days of sobriety who are willing to show up for other women here. Will you be a mentor?"

At that time the program was new, and the requirements and policies were different than they likely are today. I didn't sign my name on a dotted line, but I nodded my head.

Really? You really think I have something to offer? Doubts plagued my mind but I said yes anyway.

Yes, I'll be a mentor.

No, I don't feel ready.

And yet this is the moment when my purpose was born in recovery. When I said yes.

Our lives are like stones thrown into the sea of the world. Within this vast place we still have a place—even though the largeness of our lives feels small when we remember that our troubles and trials pale in comparison with the world's immensity.

With the many women I've mentored over the years, one thing seems to be a deciding factor in both motivation to change and likelihood of a sustained recovery: purpose. It doesn't matter if we have twenty-four hours or twenty-four years. We all need a reason to stay in recovery. To do this thing that has hard days, excruciating days. To keep on the path even if our loved ones take a while to trust us again or even as we are losing friends and loved ones to addiction way too often.

There is a saying in addiction treatment and some pathways that says we "have to get sober for us." No other reason—our kids, our jobs, our families—will help us get there.

I don't agree with this statement.

I think we *do* need a reason outside our ourselves. We need purpose.

Our lives matter. Our lives can make an impact on another human being, most often those closest to us who are a part of our inner circles, a part of our families whether biological or chosen.

Every person who is struggling with substance use, every parent who loses precious hours of sleep or sanity over them, every gracious and humble person in recovery who is motivated to help the next person struggling—all of our lives matter. We can each be that stone that glides across the water, touching lives as we go.

A friend told me recently that even if we don't see the impact we are having on another person, we may be influencing their hours for eternity. The actions we take today to love and understand and support those we hold dear—or even complete strangers who are kindred because of our shared experience—they matter. We matter.

In paying it forward and doing the next right thing we are saying a new world is possible, whether we are in recovery, trying to find our pathway, or loving someone as they search. A new life awaits. Advocates like Christina Dent and many of the other folks I've mentioned are examples of this. They are family members and loved ones who walk alongside others while they find their own paths to recovery and discover (or perhaps rediscover) their reason why.

Remember

Purpose is a central part of a sustained recovery. Family members can also find new purpose because of their loved one's recovery journeys.

Reflect

- How have you seen your loved one become purpose-driven?
- In what ways can you support their activities, work, volunteer opportunities, ministry, or other endeavors?

Chapter 15

Circle of Chairs

He became somebody I didn't recognize. It was like a stranger in the house. He didn't stick to any rules, any boundaries."

As she spoke these words pleading for help, I recognized that families need circles too.

I met Valerie Forsey on Zoom because we are thousands of miles and an ocean apart. She is an affected mother who started the organization DAFS, or Drug and Alcohol Family Support, in the UK. It's for parents and family members of loved ones impacted by addiction and aims to create a safe and welcoming environment free from judgment.

Valerie knows firsthand the importance of having a place where guidance is shared. She knows that navigating a child's addiction is like walking in the dark. DAFS says that "the most important thing is that you can feel part of a group who 'get it' and that you realize that you are not alone in all of this."[1]

When she was struggling in her own pit of despair, she admitted the depth of where her heart was, how defeated their family was. "It would be kinder to all of us if he just died. What mother can say that about their child? This for me was my light bulb moment where I just thought, that's how powerful addiction is."

Addiction was ravishing their family, but it wasn't only her son that needed help. When their son started struggling, she and her husband did not know anything about addiction. They kept telling themselves that in a few months it was going to be okay. Fear kept her from talking about it with anyone. They started isolating and fixating on their son's every move, every change. For four years it was torture.

"What will fix him?" She obsessed over this question and thought there should be an easy answer.

Valerie, like so many parents and affected family members, came to understand that it wasn't about fixing their loved one—or remaining isolated. It was learning about addiction, understanding recovery, and finding a path of meaning and purpose for themselves—adjacent to their loved one's journey, but distinctly their own.

They also came to understand that what was helpful for them was helpful for their son: support from people who had been there. In their own newfound community, Valerie shared that "the biggest thing for me was that isolation dissipated and I felt that I was able to be heard, to be seen. Not be judged."

Today Valerie's son is celebrating another year living in recovery. He is a father to his daughter, a boyfriend, an employee, and a trusted family member. And he works with people who are struggling with addiction.

Valerie's experience founding and now running DAFS was one of having eyes opened. Her family learned that there is no "fixing" their son. There is only loving, walking alongside, and learning how to support him. Importantly, it's also about learning that the whole family needs support too.

"We thought *they* were going to fix it . . . But what [connecting in community] did was it opened my eyes to the power of talking and sharing."[2]

Valerie and her husband, like so many family members and loved ones, learned an important lesson. To best support their loved one struggling, they need to discover a community of their own. A circle of chairs where they feel welcome, loved, and accepted.

The recovery community is where individuals have experienced immense struggle, but it's also where vulnerability and honesty about those challenges brings connection. In a circle of chairs, there is openness and vulnerability. There isn't blame or ultimatums, which can ostracize loved ones; there is grace and there is an invitation.

I've experienced my own version of being fully accepted into a community after I pleaded for help and let other people into the dark parts of my story. Sharing our stories in a welcoming community can help us find freedom. This can bring hope and healing. It normalizes the challenges that families face. As Jesus says in Matthew 18:20, "Where two or three gather in my name," God promises his presence.

Often it is in recovery circles where many people experience a connection with God for the first time. As John Ortberg writes in *Steps*,

> What we need is a place where it is safe to be inadequate. . . . Recovery groups are places where people know they will find genuine friendship and love precisely when they describe their weakness and struggle. People who name their addictions and relapses and firings and failures and family blow-ups and lying are actually cheered on. The worse your story, the warmer your welcome. This is not because they've done bad things, but because they have come clean about it.[3]

Open circles turn wounds to scars. Together, we learn how to share from the "healing and not the bleeding," as I've heard wise storytellers say.

Whether we identify as being in or seeking recovery or having affected loved ones, recovery communities are where we can show up as ourselves with our flaws, hurts, hang-ups, relationship challenges, failures, and regrets. We can share our dirt and know that what will be shared back is not always advice or counsel, but a listening ear.

A head nod.

A *yes* and *amen.*

A *we've been there.*

A *me too.*

There are many affected family members and loved ones (this might be you) who have walked the road—sometimes along a sustained recovery for their loved one and sometimes through tragedy—and are moved to help others through the power of the circle, the power of vulnerable sharing and community like Valerie.

What I love about this is that it doesn't matter where we are coming from or how we are identifying (as an affected family member or person in recovery or doubter or seeker). Our stories can speak to one another when we listen.

I love what family recovery advocate and coach Timothy Harrington shares: "It's not out here where you don't have—that's not your influence. Your influence is your ability to connect, your natural nurturing, your natural interest and curiosity and desire for change." Our stories can influence and impact. Sometimes it's from a circle of chairs that our next step in recovery is born and our newfound purpose is unleashed.

Do you remember the story from William Cope Moyers that I shared at the beginning of this book? I'd like to end this chapter with a few more brief stories and reflections from affected family members and loved ones. These are all answers to this question: "What is family recovery?" As you read the answers, notice how giving back is tied to each one.

- "Family recovery means creating a space where each family member can heal, grow, and reconnect. It's about building resilience, understanding, and open communication so the entire family can move forward together, healthier and stronger."
- "Healing, unity, and forgiveness."
- "Growth and empathy with the understanding that we all play some role in this family disease, regardless of how infinite or

large. It would mean I can sleep at night. It would mean my grandchildren would get their parent back. It would mean a healthier life for my loved one. We are the missing piece of the puzzle for a successful recovery as family, especially for the individual needing empathy, support, and time to heal! This is not an easy fix. Recovery time is lengthy!"

- "Addiction is a family disease. Family goes through a lot of psychological, emotional, social turmoil while dealing with a person with SUD. Addiction doesn't just affect the individual; it disrupts the dynamics, relationships, and emotional well-being of the entire family system. Family recovery involves addressing these impacts while fostering a supportive, understanding, and healthier environment."
- "Family recovery to me means including all available and willing family members in SUD treatment, both because we are all impacted and because we can all have an influence on the success or challenges of our loved ones."
- "Family recovery means that both the family member and the peer understand what recovery means and why they can make better decisions if they are in recovery. The information given to the family member is shared with the parent or caregiver so that they can move through recovery together. Each can support the other."

Recovery is about being of service. It is about a giving of ourselves. And it is about doing this together.

This pouring forth may happen while sitting in a support meeting of our own. It might happen as we share and listen or provide support. It might happen through actively listening, loving, and empathizing with our loved one. For both affected loved ones and those of us in recovery, the journey is one of finding new purpose in not only sharing our stories but in living out our stories together.

Remember

Honesty and vulnerability can bring amazing movements of healing through the recovery community.

Reflect

- How have you been moved by community and connection or perhaps a support group or family recovery meetings?
- If you have not yet experienced this, are you willing to try?
- Where are the local family recovery meetings or support groups in your community?

Conclusion

Recovery Is for Everyone

In *Finding My Way Home,* Henri Nouwen references a story about a rabbi who asks a question of his students: "How can we determine the hour of dawn, when the night ends and the day begins?"[1]

His students replied with two questions:

"When from a distance you can distinguish between a dog and a sheep?"

And the teacher replied, "No."

"Is it when one can distinguish between a fig tree and a grapevine?"

Again the teacher replied, "No."

The students begged for the rabbi to share the correct answer, and my guess is that they started to assume this was headed in a bit deeper direction than they had expected.

Finally the teacher gave them the answer: "When you can look into the face of another human being and you have enough light in you to recognize your brother or your sister. Until then it is night, and darkness is still with us."

When we can move from feeling *different than* to *part of.*

When we can halt the lie that "I am not like you" and mean it.

When we can look at our loved one and look in the mirror and look with compassion into the eyes staring back at us.

When we can recognize, as the Jewish teacher shared, that we can move from a place of darkness to one of light, when we see that we are all God's children—all deserving of love, all needing a *welcome home* of our own. That is when we can come to a new understanding of our loved one's journey through addiction and into recovery. We can bring the tools and skills we've learned to build trust, foster safety, and meet our loved ones with compassion and empathy. A new light can shine into the night.

My hope for you is that you can recognize this light when you look at your loved one.

No matter where they are on their journey, whether in abstinence-based recovery for decades, practicing harm reduction, or still in the early stages of navigating what it means to want to change course or take another path, what may help your loved one the most and provide the most support is *you being there.*

With boundaries, yes.

Saying no at times, yes.

Distancing with love when they are using, perhaps.

But with an open heart? Yes.

Believing in hope? Yes.

Trusting that change is coming? Always.

Knowing that just your love and acceptance can make a difference? Absolutely.

Remember: Recovery is hope, wellness, community, and service.

Recovery Is Hope

Hope is the foundation of recovery, both for those of us in or seeking recovery and our loved ones. Believing in healing and transformation increases the chances of long-term recovery. Understanding the neuroscience of addiction and recovery addresses and then decreases stigma, helping everyone more fully understand the recovery process and its innumerable pathways.

Recovery Is Wellness

Recovery goes beyond abstinence—it's about overall well-being. Physical, emotional, and spiritual health play key roles in long-term healing. Many of us in recovery find that improving physical health strengthens our resilience. Addressing our mental health leads to greater quality of life. And growing in our spiritual health can help us deepen our faith. True wellness involves a holistic approach that nurtures the mind, body, and spirit.

Recovery Is Community

Recovery is not a solo journey—it thrives in connection. Support groups, faith communities, and advocacy opportunities and networks can create a supportive family where healing flourishes. Openly sharing recovery stories encourages others to seek help. A strong community helps everyone, including affected family members, navigate the recovery process together.

Recovery Is Service

Purpose is central to sustained recovery. Supporting loved ones in finding meaning—through volunteer work, advocacy, or creative outlets—strengthens our healing journey and can have long-term and lasting positive health effects. Many of us in recovery become leaders who serve and are committed to living lives of meaning and purpose, sharing our stories and creating spaces for others to heal.

You, dear reader, can be a part of this journey of recovery, which guides us into pathways that can turn our darkness into light. And what a beautiful thing to witness *when the light comes back*. When the road of recovery leads us back home to ourselves, to our families, to community.

I've experienced it. My family is experiencing it. Millions of families around the globe are living in recovery. We all "have a place in recovery, because recovery is for everyone."[2] My hope for you is that you and your loved one can too. Let us believe until it is true and then always hang on to hope.

As my friends in recovery like to say, "Don't give up before the miracle happens."

Remember

Recovery is for family members. Recovery is for those of us in or seeking wholeness and healing. Recovery is for everyone.

Reflect

- How are you prompted to begin a recovery journey?
- In what ways is recovery for you too?
- What is next for your journey?

A Note on Grief

The first time we met, our church was hosting a women's event for the recovery ministry. It was at a local tea shop where everything was pink and floral and more than Instagram friendly. There were kitschy decorations and trendy bubble teas, and the owners had agreed to host our group of ladies from nearby treatment centers, transitional housing, and recovery housing.

Elyse walked in and I instantly recognized her. The sad, hollow eyes. The way her black hoodie was up over her head and almost touching her lashes, where days-old mascara crusted under her eyes. Everything about her screamed "I don't want to be here. I don't want to be anywhere anymore."

I recognized her because I was her at so many points in my life. One was the moment when my dad pulled me close to him and I sank into the realization that I needed to change, wanted to change, or I might not make it.

She was tired.

I would find out later that she never wanted to go to the Christmas women's event that day. It was her first day—her very first day—off the streets and starting recovery. I nestled my way close to her as some of the women who'd been around a bit longer laughed and sipped tea and opened gifts.

"You are loved," the church said by passing out gift bags with face masks and plush socks and sweet-smelling lotions.

Elyse began to relax the longer she was there. Her jaw unclenched. Her knee stopped bouncing. She talked to me when

I asked her what brought her to our small town, and tears welled in her eyes.

"I can't live like this anymore. But I'm scared," she said.

The first time Elyse entered this particular pink-laden tea shop in East Tennessee, it was a welcome home (though she may not have recognized it at the time).

It was a *you belong* and a *you are welcome here* and a *you have found your people.*

Elyse was set lovingly in a recovery family.

As she began to trust me and the other women around her, and as she started seeing a therapist and getting support for not just her addiction but also other challenges, she began to bloom. Once hidden under her hoodie, now her eyes were lined in blue liner. She wore floral blouses and her hair was as dark as the black stones I remember seeing in Alaska once. She carried her Bible and went to church and started working again.

As Elyse shared her story with me by living in community with me and others, I saw what we often see in recovery: Our stories are mirrors and windows. They are a reflecting back and an inviting in.

Elyse's story was my story too.

And Heather's story. Amanda's story. Alex's story.

Amy's story. Kristi's story. Elisabeth's story.

All the women she met in recovery—we understood each other. She showed me what recovery looked like. And not just recovery, but hope and faith and perseverance. God would continue to set Elyse in recovery families who loved and cared for her—and she loved and cared for us.

When I was writing the first draft of this book, I got the kind of text that you want to un-get as soon as you look: "Elyse died."

I was prepping dinner, chopping something or stirring, I can't remember now.

My head and stomach dropped.

No.

Not her.

Not again.

What I shared above is part of what I shared at her funeral after her mother asked that I say a few words. I wore purple like her nine-year-old daughter. My hands shook as I held the pages with my scribbled words.

After I sat back down and listened to one of Elyse's favorite songs, I closed my eyes and then opened them and stared at the urn. Stared at the pictures of her with her daughter. Looked at the large framed photograph that the family had chosen. Her hair was golden blonde and her eyes looked happy, how they looked when she had been in recovery and not using. In my mind I heard her laughing. A child happy again. At peace.

Elyse has now experienced a new kind of welcome home. And I am glad, though I miss her and though she should still be here.

You may know this pain. You may be reading these pages because you work in recovery or have started an organization to support family members because you've lost your child or another loved one. Perhaps you are like me and have been to too many funerals to count.

My friend Honesty Liller from the McShin Foundation says that she has picture frames in her office of those she's lost and it's been hundreds of funerals that she has had to go to. Hundreds.

We are not ending here, but I can't share a book about what recovery is without acknowledging the hard truth that so many families face or the fear that so many live with. When our loved ones are misusing substances or have substance use disorder, especially in today's world, sometimes it is like playing a game of Russian roulette. One more time might be our loved one's last. Or for some families, their loved one's first time using a substance is their last mistake.

The reality is so heartbreaking that words fail me here. Death and grief are a part of the recovery journey. If we don't lose our loved ones from addiction (and I so pray and hope that we don't have to suffer this tragedy), we are guaranteed to lose those we love at some point along the path.

The road we walk on or trudge in recovery does have mountaintop experiences. Moments of health and wellness physically, mentally, and spiritually. Connections in community and opportunities to be of service that fill us with newfound purpose and perseverance. But then there are those moments death brings that threaten to derail us. Our minds sometimes offering the option to "go back out," as if using again could bring them back or help ease the pain. Grief can threaten to swallow us in anger or sadness or guilt or regret.

Recovery can be hard. It is hard to feel. To show up. To live without a crutch or blinders that tune out the world around us—the grief and the good stuff. But it is so much more real when we show up. When we can show up for all of it.

When the pastor called and asked if I could share a few words at Elyse's funeral after her sudden death, I said yes. I was alert. Aware. *Ready*. We can continue on this road even when it aches. When it aches, we have each other.

If you are a family member who has lost a loved one, my heart aches for you. However you show up as you are reading these pages, I want you to know, you aren't alone. If your loved one didn't make it, but you are still here, still reading these words, still reaching out to understand and support those of us in or seeking addiction recovery, thank you. We need you.

Thank you for continuing to show up through your own grief, perhaps propelled by it.

Thank you for honoring the memory of your loved one and keeping their light alive by helping others on this path. Many of us (I'm raising my hand) have been held up, our own lights illumined by the shadows of tears and grief from a mom or dad or sister or brother or neighbor or friend who has been crushed by addiction loss and found purpose in working to keep others from experiencing the same pain.

Thank you.

You've saved my life. You've saved so many of our lives.

Grief is universal. While it might be easier to forget that death can be a part of the recovery journey, it is important that we remember and honor the stories of loved ones who have experienced tragedy. Pam Lanhart is someone I've met through my advocacy work. She is the founder of a recovery community for affected family members in Minnesota called Thrive Recovery. This is her family's story.

Pam's Story

"You need to come and get your son. He showed up to school with a backpack full of pills." Jake was in seventh grade and just thirteen years old.

We had seen the signs. You know the ones. Matches in his pocket. Small amounts of missing money. Times where I would go in his room and check on him and his bed would be empty.

But this . . .

We had read the books *What to Expect When You're Expecting* and *What to Expect with Your Toddler*. But we hadn't read the book *What to Expect When Your Thirteen-Year-Old Is Using Drugs*.

Looking back at the history of our family, we knew it was a possibility. Both my mom and my dad had struggled with alcohol use. We had uncles and cousins and siblings who had struggled, now all in recovery, who were plagued with mental health and substance use issues. We were educated on addiction and how it could impact future generations. We had done our homework, learned what we could, and believed all the parenting books and information that said, "If you do X, Y, and Z, you can prevent your child from going down the wrong path."

But this . . .

We also knew that Jake was at a high risk. From the moment he was born he was an extraordinary child. He was a contradiction of personality—both anxious and a risk-taker at the same time. He self-soothed by sucking his thumb until he was about twelve, needing the comfort that brought into his body. Yet he was fearless and reckless.

When we couldn't find Jake at any given moment, we simply had to look up to find him. He climbed everything, jumped off anything higher than he was. And despite his small stature, he would stand up to anyone, anytime if he thought they were wronging him. He was fierce on the football or rugby field, tackling opposing players that were twice or three times his weight.

But this. What do you do when you have a thirteen-year-old smoking marijuana?

If you followed our initial protocols you do everything that you *aren't* supposed to do. We defaulted immediately to our "make it stop" behaviors.

Step 1: Get him even more involved in risk-taking activities. So instead of playing football where he could get kicked off the team, we moved on to mountain biking, MMA, and eventually rugby.

Step 2: Become hypervigilant and monitor every single thing that he is doing. Track his whereabouts, check in with the families he spent time with, take his phone away, check his phone when he had it.

Step 3: Lecture and talk, talk and lecture until our voices were hoarse and we were exhausted from the chaos and conflict that was a daily part of our lives. None of these tactics worked, of course. While they gave us some short-term satisfaction that we were doing "something," what we know now is that most of the things we did simply made things worse and caused harm in our relationship.

The other thing that happened is that we began to dehumanize our son. We treated him as we saw him, like a "bad" kid, rather than treating him like the person that we thought he could grow up to be. That led to lots of behaviors that involved lecturing, telling, blaming, and shaming him. If I had a dollar for every man-to-man talk that my husband had with my son, in hopes that he might change, we would be wealthy individuals.

At the young age of just fifteen, Jake went into his first treatment. It is a nationally renowned program that has an incredible reputation for leading people into recovery. I remember a counselor looking us in the eyes and with as much compassion as he could muster, saying to us, "You know your son could die from this disease." While we had hoped that this treatment experience would be a one-and-done situation, as it turned out, it was just the beginning.

Over the next few years our son's use escalated, and our feelings of helplessness grew deeper. We were told that we were powerless, that there was nothing we could do and that we had to "disconnect," "detach," and "let him hit rock bottom," which was absolutely terrifying as we began to see overdose deaths start to rise during the time we were fighting the hardest to get our son help.

Not long after his first treatment experience, he ended up in trouble with the law and was charged with a felony: breaking and entering. We felt we had no other choice but to support the narratives of taking a punitive approach to fighting his addiction. And as we tried to navigate his behaviors, our relationship deteriorated more and more.

During that challenging time two things happened as a result of his criminal justice involvement, both of which changed our lives. The first was that our son was given the option of a diversion program, which involved juvenile treatment court. During that time we were exposed to family dialectical behavioral therapy, which began to equip us with necessary communication skills. We also saw the power of creating a "wrap team," which offered a scaffolding of support that involved not just the entire family system but also other robust supports including mentors, school counselors, social workers, and of course a probation officer. It was a true, visual example of how the system should work for people who have problematic behaviors that are a direct result of their substance use.

The second thing that happened was that as we began to engage in the changes we needed to make in order to support him, we were convicted more and more that we had to take a serious look at our own behaviors and how we were interacting with our son. During that time, we met with a pastoral counselor and discussed our situation. We wanted to show up for our son in a way that aligned with our values.

Our intention was that we would walk out character attributes like kindness, compassion, empathy, and love. Most of the time, our behaviors didn't match our intentions. We were activated, angry, fearful, distraught, impatient, and very shaming toward our "addict" son. As we sat in front of this counselor, in total desperation, he made a profound statement that would change the rest of our lives. I wrote down his words and they are taped to my bedroom mirror to this day: "Are you going to be right for the sake of justice or love for the sake of relationship? Because love never fails, and justice was already paid for on the cross."

Breaking that down in a very simplistic way looked like, "Are you going to be right, or are you going to love right?" We had tried to force ourselves on our son to move him to recovery. But in reality, all it did was drive us further away due to judgment, unrealistic expectations, and loads of resentment.

As we left that office, I knew that I had to change. I had to "be done." And I was done, but not in the way that you would expect. As I look back, that was the day that I truly began to work my own recovery program.

I was done instigating confrontation. I began to learn how to respond to my son with compassion, understanding, and unconditional, positive regard rather than dehumanizing him and creating conflict and chaos.

I was done treating my son like he was bad rather than ill. And I began to get educated about substance use, to see that my son's behaviors made sense and that he was just trying to feel better and mitigate his own pain. I began to learn that his substance use had actually changed his brain, created new neuropathways, and formed deeply rooted instinctual behaviors. For him, to use was to breathe and to sustain life.

I was done taking the behaviors of the disease personally. And I began to self-differentiate. His behaviors were not about me. And when I learned to separate my son, who I knew as a human, from the addiction that was consuming him, I was able to respond differently.

I was done behaving in a way that didn't match my values. When I really looked at my way of being and the energy that I was sending to my son, I had to admit that I was a big part of the problem.

When I began to look at my own trauma, my own ways that I was activated, and most importantly how I was modeling health and well-being, things started changing. I began to learn how to pause and how to self-regulate so I could make decisions aligned with my values.

I was done putting the addiction in the center of our family and letting it consume every ounce of my time, energy, and mental capacity. And I began finding joy in other relationships, investing in my marriage and my relationships with our other children.

I was done feeling powerless. And I began to discover all the important things that I could do to help myself and learn how to show up differently in my life. Things like creating healthy routines, taking care of my mental and emotional health, being consistent with my spiritual practices, giving back to my community, and walking out my own mission and purpose.

As I began to do my work and heal from a life of personal trauma, my relationship with our son also began to heal and repair. Recovery for me, as a family member, was about returning to my own health and well-being and reclaiming all the things that I had lost not just as a result of our son's addiction but going all the way back to my life as a child with parents who had both struggled with substance misuse.

During the next six years, while our son's journey was rough and jagged, we were able to connect in deep and meaningful ways. We had healing conversations, we made repairs, and most importantly we had fun together. We climbed mountains, both literally and metaphorically.

I wish that I could say that this story had a perfect ending. During a short return to use in October of 2021 after the isolation and challenges during COVID-19, our son lost his life to an accidental overdose.

So how do you find hope in this story? When I look at our grief journey and how we have walked through the last three years of our lives, the gift we have is the gift of our personal recovery, as well as the beauty of repair and of no regrets. This is recovery. Living our lives in a way that when we look back, regardless of outcomes, we have the assurance that we have walked through life in the most honoring way possible. Honoring our journey, honoring our faith, and most importantly, honoring our son.

Pam's story might be your story, and if this is the case, my heart breaks for you. No parent or loved one should ever have to lose someone they love to addiction.

If your world is hurting, I want to encourage you to reach out for support. Organizations like Pam's can provide support from people who are walking in your shoes. We never have to do life alone.

Resources

The following is a collection of resources, including a glossary of key terms, recommended reading, and exercises to help support you when you love someone in or seeking recovery. Each resource will provide you with something different to expand on. You are the expert of your life. You have unique experiences, insights, and stories that can help your own adaptation of what's helpful for you and your family or relationships.

I'd also love to hear from you about what was helpful or if you'd like to see anything added to this collection. At the end of the book is more information on how to get in touch with me. We are in this together.

Helpful Exercises

Take Our Thoughts (and Responses) for a Walk

This exercise is adapted from the book *Beyond Addiction*.[1] We can focus all our attention and energy on our loved one's substance use or recovery—or we can shift our focus on what we *can* control. This exercise is meant to help us as loved ones and affected family members look at our own thinking as it relates to recovery.

In each of the three columns, write down a specific action (either a personal action or one done by our loved one), triggers that may have precipitated that action, and then any results. You can look back on this over time and work with a therapist or other trusted support to shift how you respond.

Here is an example:

Actions	Triggers	Results	Response
Anger driven by fear. I got upset with my friend who is using substances problematically.	My friend had a recurrence of use after one year of recovery.	I'm afraid that their recovery is not real since they relapsed.	As a response, I know that I can take action to join a peer support group to talk about my experience and learn more about the science of addiction. Recurrence of use can be a normal part of the recovery process.

Recovery Capital Measure

This assessment is a way to measure where you are on a continuum in terms of support, and it is adapted from decades of research.[2] It helps you identify strengths and areas of support needs for your loved one. This sample assessment is a way for family members to help loved ones identify, develop, build, and maintain capital.* If there are areas missing where more recovery capital is needed, more focus can be spent encouraging these areas or for our loved ones to take action toward them.

Recovery capital isn't just for our loved ones. Everyone can benefit from identifying those strengths, skills, and assets where more growth or support is needed.

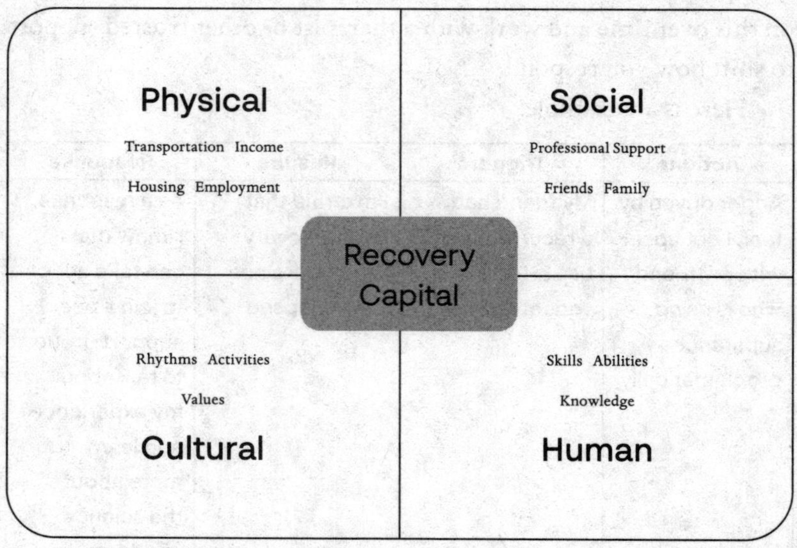

* Another excellent tool for measuring recovery capital is the Multidimensional Inventory of Recovery Capital (MIRC): https://socialwork.buffalo.edu/resources/multidimensional-inventory-recovery-capital.html.

Family and Loved Ones Recovery Mind-Set Tool

Mind-set is key for a healthy and sustained recovery. This tool is meant to support you to be an empowered partner alongside your loved one. In recovery, we heal together. This tool includes reflective questions, ideas for positive reinforcement, and actionable mind-set shifts that can encourage both your loved one and hopefully you!

Start Here: Self-Reflection Matters

Supporting someone in recovery is tough. It's also powerful. To support our loved ones in healthy ways, we can begin by asking ourselves these questions:

- How am I supporting my loved one's recovery—emotionally, practically, and spiritually?
- Am I giving them space to grow or stepping in too much out of fear?
- Have I taken time to understand addiction as a disease—not a moral failure?
- Have I taken time to understand recovery as a holistic concept that includes not just sobriety or abstinence but other elements like physical, mental, and spiritual well-being?
- Am I taking care of my own well-being while supporting them?

Reflective Questions to Promote Family Recovery

The following are examples of questions that you can use to reflect on your own support. Remember, reflection can be most helpful when done in a supportive and loving community. You can use these prompts regularly—alone, with a counselor, or in family support groups:

Emotional Support

- What does my loved one need from me today—encouragement, listening, or space?
- How do I respond when they're struggling—do I react or respond with compassion?
- Am I celebrating their small wins?

Communication

- Do I speak with love and clarity, or with fear and frustration?
- Am I asking open-ended questions like "How can I support you today?" instead of giving advice?

Boundaries and Self-Care

- What boundaries have I set that support their healing and protect my peace?
- Am I attending to my own emotional health or losing myself in their problematic substance use, addiction, or recovery?

Example Questions to Build Connection and Trust

The following are meant to be starting points or examples of questions that you can use in conversations with your loved one to spark openness and reduce shame:

- What's been the most exciting part of your recovery lately?
- What's been the hardest part of your recovery lately?
- How can we make our home feel like a safe place for your healing?
- What's one thing you need from me this week?
- I'm proud of how you handled today. Can we talk about it?

Celebrate the Small Wins

Celebrating milestones is a fun and helpful way to encourage ongoing recovery. Every positive choice deserves recognition, not just the big milestones like sobriety birthdays, although these are super fun to recognize too.

You can try phrases like

- I saw how you paused before reacting—that's growth.
- I'm really proud of how honest you were just now.
- You didn't give up when it got hard. That's huge.
- Thank you for letting me in. That means a lot.

Remember: Recovery is about progress, not perfection. Setbacks don't mean failure—they can be just another step on the journey or even help to propel us to what's next. Healing is also a family process. Our own growth and even our own recovery is key.

Additional Key Points to Consider*

- **Families can help their loved ones:** Involving families increases the likelihood of engaging in treatment and recovery support services.
- **Helping ourselves helps too:** Self-care for family members is crucial; it models self-care to loved ones and helps family members show up in healthier ways.
- **Addiction is normal:** Substance use and disorders impact almost all families today; we shouldn't feel different for dealing with addiction or supporting recovery.
- **Reframing is key to understanding and compassion:** Changing how we talk about loved ones promotes a more empathetic and compassionate view.

* Copy these and tape them to your bathroom mirror or office computer. You could even tattoo one on your forearm! Just kidding (sort of).

- **Treatment isn't the only way to get better:** Good treatment often includes psychiatric care; substance problems are complex and require specialized attention beyond just stopping substance use.
- **Resistance to change is normal:** Ambivalence is a normal part of the change process; black-and-white thinking in treatment settings can be ineffective.
- **Change is possible:** As long as everyone is still breathing, change is possible; willingness to change is key.

Key Terms

Here is a list of key terms to be mindful of when loving someone in recovery. Language is always changing, with new terms being added when the science or our stories inform important updates in terminology. As with all things, test what is still good, and be ready to keep learning and add to this list over time. At the end there is space for you to add your own key terms as you continue on this journey with your loved one.

Abstinence: Refraining from substance use entirely.

Addiction: A chronic condition characterized by compulsive drug seeking, continued use despite harmful consequences, and long-lasting changes in the brain. In some circles the word *addiction* itself is considered stigmatizing. Some prefer using the term *substance use disorder* or *problematic substance use*. Always ask your loved one how they prefer to refer to this and other concepts.

Alcoholics Anonymous (AA): A fellowship of individuals who share their experiences, strength, and hope to solve their common problem and help others recover from alcoholism. There are many different types of *A*'s since the advent of AA, including NA (Narcotics Anonymous), OA (Overeater's Anonymous), and MA (Marijuana Anonymous), just to name a few.

Al-Anon: Al-Anon, short for Al-Anon Family Groups, follows the 12 steps of AA and is a worldwide support group designed for friends and families of individuals who struggle with alcohol addiction. It operates on the principle that alcoholism affects not just the person who drinks but also their loved ones. Al-Anon provides a safe and confidential environment where people can share their experiences, seek support, and gain strength from others who understand their situation. The goal is to help participants find peace, healing, and a way to regain control of their own lives, regardless of their loved one's sustained recovery or return to use.

Buprenorphine: A medication used to treat opioid addiction by reducing withdrawal symptoms and cravings.

Case Management: Services provided to assist and support individuals in gaining access to needed medical, social, educational, and other services.

Ceiling Effect: The phenomenon in which a drug reaches a maximum effect so that increasing the drug dosage does not increase its effectiveness.

Codependency: Traditionally seen as a dysfunctional relationship where one person supports or enables another person's addiction. More accurately, this is a relational state where there are unhealthy boundaries and an emotional responsibility by the loved one that can be detrimental to everyone involved, including themselves.

Cognitive Behavioral Therapy (CBT): A type of psychotherapy that helps individuals change negative thought patterns and behaviors.

Delirium Tremens (DTs): Severe alcohol withdrawal symptoms including shaking, confusion, and hallucinations. Alcohol withdrawal symptoms can be fatal and usually require prompt medical attention.

Detoxification (Detox): The process of removing toxic substances from the body.

Dual Diagnosis: The co-occurrence of a substance use disorder and a mental health disorder.

Emotional Sobriety: Beyond physical abstinence, this refers to the emotional balance, resilience, and self-awareness that supports long-term recovery. Emotional sobriety is also a part of healthy relationships in recovery.

Family Therapy: Therapy that involves family members in the treatment process.

Group Therapy: Therapy that involves multiple individuals working together with a therapist.

Harm Reduction: Strategies aimed at reducing the negative consequences of drug use without necessarily stopping the use itself.

Individual Therapy: One-on-one therapy sessions with a therapist.

Inpatient Treatment: Treatment that takes place in a residential facility.

Intervention: This is a structured meeting often facilitated by a trained interventionist, where loved ones confront someone struggling with addiction or problematic substance use and encourage them to make the choice to go to treatment.

Medication-Assisted Treatment (MAT): The use of medications, in combination with counseling and behavioral therapies, to treat substance use disorders. Some believe that the use of this treatment option is "substituting one drug for another"; however, the use of MAT is an evidence-based way for many individuals to find and sustain long-term recovery.

Motivational Interviewing (MI): A counseling approach that helps individuals find the motivation to make positive changes.

Multiple Pathways: Refers to the idea that there isn't just one way to find or maintain sobriety or recovery. Recovery can be an individualized process and change depending on the stage of recovery or season of life.

Naloxone: A medication used to reverse opioid overdoses.

Naltrexone: A medication used to prevent relapse in individuals with opioid or alcohol dependence.

Outpatient Treatment: Treatment that takes place on an outpatient basis, allowing individuals to live at home.

Partial Hospitalization Program (PHP): A structured program that provides intensive treatment during the day but allows individuals to return home at night.

Peer Support: Support provided by individuals who have experienced similar challenges and can offer guidance and encouragement. This type of support can be found in both informal relationships and structured roles like Certified Peer Recovery Specialists.

Post-Acute Withdrawal Syndrome (PAWS): Ongoing withdrawal symptoms such as anxiety, irritability, or interrupted sleep or insomnia that may persist after the acute detox phase, sometimes for months.

Protective Factors: These are conditions or attributes (like strong support systems, faith, or coping skills) that reduce risk and increase resilience during recovery.

Recovery: This is a way of life that is about more than sobriety or a journey of abstinence from alcohol or other drug use. It is about a wellness mind-set that incorporates a focus on maintaining and strengthening physical, mental, and spiritual health, along with living a life of service in community with others.

Recovery Capital: The resources someone needs to support their recovery journey. It includes internal strengths and external supports that include personal, social, cultural, and community-based elements.

Recovery Coach: A person who provides support and guidance to individuals in recovery. This is a nonclinical role, but the individual goes through a rigorous training curriculum and often supervision before working independently with individuals.

Rehabilitation (Rehab): A program designed to help individuals recover from substance use disorders.

Relapse: The return to substance use after an attempt to stop. Because of the negative connotation many have with the term *relapse*, the non-stigmatizing phrase *return to use* is replacing it. Return to use can be a normal part of the recovery process, although sustained, long-term recovery and abstinence is possible—and probable when we have the support and resources we need.

Seeking Recovery: This is a way to describe individuals who may still be involved in problematic substance use.

Self-Help Groups: Groups where individuals with similar experiences come together to support each other.

Sober Companion: A person who provides support and companionship to individuals in recovery.

Sober Living House: A supportive living environment for individuals in recovery. This can also be called a recovery residence or recovery home. In some places, the different terms for these housing options have different levels of care, approaches, or policies.

Stigma: Negative beliefs or attitudes toward individuals with substance use disorder and those in recovery. Stigma can also lead to discriminatory behaviors, practices, and policies such as the "not in my own backyard" attitudes of people who don't want recovery housing or treatment facilities in their neighborhoods. Reducing stigma helps create a more compassionate, supportive recovery environment.

Substance Use Disorder (SUD): A medical condition characterized by an inability to stop using a substance despite negative consequences.

Support Group: A group of individuals who come together to support each other in their recovery journey. There are innumerable types of support groups. Small groups in faith communities can operate similarly to many recovery support groups too.

Therapeutic Community (TC): A structured environment where individuals in recovery live and work together to support each other's recovery.

Tolerance: The need to use more of a substance to achieve the same effect.

Transitional Living: A transitional living environment is a supportive, structured setting designed to help individuals bridge the gap between intensive treatment and independent living.

Trauma-Informed Care: An evidence-based treatment approach that acknowledges the impact of past trauma and prioritizes enhancing safety, trustworthiness and authentic engagement, and empowerment in the healing process.

Treatment: Addiction and mental health treatment involve a variety of approaches, modalities, and evidence-based practices. They are meant to do more than treat substance use challenges or mental health symptoms. Quality treatment addresses the underlying root causes and provides a starting point for a successful and sustained road of recovery. For most individuals, it takes more than one type of treatment over time to address underlying causes and provide needed support. Treatment can include medical detox, outpatient, inpatient, residential, and medication-assisted options.

Triggers: Situations, people, or events that can lead to cravings and sometimes a potential recurrence of use.

12-Step Programs: A set of guiding principles for recovery from addiction, originally developed by Alcoholics Anonymous.

Urine Drug Screen (UDS): A test used to detect the presence of drugs in a person's urine. Referring to the results as *clean* or *dirty* can be seen as stigmatizing language. Using *positive* or *negative* can be a more helpful way to describe the medical results of this test.

Withdrawal: Symptoms that occur after stopping or reducing intake of a substance. Alcohol withdrawal, opioid withdrawal, and other types of substance withdrawal can require medical care and intervention.

Withdrawal Management: The process of helping individuals safely manage withdrawal symptoms.

There are other terms that you will find are important to your loved one and your journey. Add your own key terms below, or use the space to make notes about changing or updating definitions.

____

____

____

____

Recovery Pathways

If the term *pathways* leads you to think "winding roads," perhaps (if you are an aging millennial like myself) you may get a Sheryl Crow song stuck in your head. For those born after 2002, just keep reading.

I'd like to demystify the concept of recovery pathways because for many family members, including my own husband, I've had to explain what the options are for people in or seeking recovery.

There are many roads that can lead us to wellness. Here are a few available to us and our loved ones. This is not an exhaustive list, but it builds on things we've already discussed, including types of recovery capital.

I'm going to structure the pathways on a continuum of support. The idea of a continuum is that it is also a process, a fluid movement from one wave to the next. Contrary to what many see as the traditional progression of recovery (prevention, treatment, recovery), this larger view incorporates other areas.

Prevention

Education Programs: There are school-based programs that provide students with information about the risks of substance use and strategies to make healthy choices. These include programs like Rise Together, which educates students about substance use and empowers them to be allies and support peers who are struggling. The US Department of Education has a wide range of webinars and other resources, including the Talk, They Hear You campaign for parents and caregivers.[1]

Community Initiatives: Many local campaigns promote drug-free activities and healthy lifestyles. SAMHSA is a federal agency that includes different initiatives to help spread awareness, like National Prevention Week during the month of May. Globally, groups like the Colombo Plan have created The Engaging Youth in Drug Use Prevention Training designed to "empower youth with the necessary knowledge and skills to proactively drive positive change and advocate for healthier lifestyles for themselves and their peers in their communities."[2]

Parenting Workshops: There are impactful and evidence-based programs that equip parents with skills and knowledge to prevent substance use among their children. Be a Part of the Conversation has a series of courses and peer support groups (see Resources for Families).[3] Among their courses are several for parents to understand and learn more about addiction recovery. Many nonprofit organizations are finding new ways to equip parents to be a part of the conversation of how to prevent substance use.

Intervention

Formal Interventions: These are structured meetings led and facilitated by a trained and licensed professional interventionist, when family and friends confront a loved one about their addiction. I have a good friend whose job is to meet people at their homes, jobs, or the airport once they've agreed to go to treatment. She then accompanies them from the moment of intervention until they walk through the doors of the treatment facility. There may also be intervention after treatment to provide recovery coaching and peer support.

Brief Interventions or Assessments: A wide range of assessment tools have been created and validated for the SUD intervention. Usually assessments are voluntary and initiated by the individual—or the parents or caregivers in the case of children or youth. An evidence-based example is SBIRT—Screening, Brief Intervention, and Referral to Treatment.[4] This is a holistic and thorough approach to providing early intervention and assessment of an individual's SUD or substance misuse. This can be done at a wide range of locations including emergency rooms, schools, with therapists, and more. For families, there are brief interventions that you can do to ascertain what level of support your family member may need.

Motivational Interviewing (MI): This counseling approach can help individuals find their motivation to change harmful behaviors. MI has traditionally been incorporated in treatment settings but has also expanded into training for peer support professionals and other care providers, including recovery coaches. MI has some helpful concepts and techniques that can be applied to communicating with and listening to our loved ones. Keep reading, and you will find practical ways to talk with and listen to your loved one in or seeking recovery.

Employee Assistance Programs (EAPs): Workplace resources like EAPs can offer confidential support and referrals for addiction treatment. There are also initiatives called "Recovery Friendly Workplaces" that provide additional recovery-centric support. The State of New Hampshire has implemented this approach, which has led to innovative support within state governments and businesses to promote recovery in the workplace, moving beyond the traditional notion of intervention.[5]

Harm Reduction

Needle Exchange Programs: Services provide clean needles to reduce the risk of infectious disease transmission. Many of these programs have been met with severe stigma due to a lack of understanding of their efficacy and the research behind them that shows how these programs lead to more people accessing treatment and point toward greater longer-term success.

Naloxone Distribution: Programs that provide naloxone to reverse opioid overdoses are a part of reducing the harm caused by substance use. For many, the risk of overdose fatality is high, especially after recurrences of use or incarceration, when tolerance levels are down. Drugs like fentanyl have also led to substance use becoming a game of Russian roulette, where *one time* can be someone's last.

Safe Injection or Consumption Sites: These are supervised spaces where individuals can use substances more safely and access health services. While not commonplace in the US and highly stigmatized, these pathways have led to a lower overdose fatality rate and greater access to treatment rate for many families. Insite in Vancouver, Canada, is North America's first legal supervised injection site. Research proves its efficacy with 35 percent fewer overdose deaths within less than a half mile radius of the program.

Along with safe injection, the center offers other types of healthcare services like primary health care and addiction treatment. It is often the first place where people are offered help for their addiction. Safe injection sites have been common practice across Europe since the 1980s in cities like Copenhagen in Denmark, Amsterdam in the Netherlands, and Zurich in Switzerland. Overdose prevention is just one of the proven facets of these sites, along with reducing disease transmission.

Over the past several years sites have been popping up along the East Coast, such as in New York City's East Harlem and Washington Heights neighborhoods. These are "a bold and contested response to a storm tide of opioid overdose deaths nationwide."[6] While critics are vocal about their disagreement with safe injection or consumption sites, the people benefiting from these services and recovery pathways are clear. Sam Rivera, the executive director of OnPoint NYC, shares that "it's a loving environment where people can use safely and stay alive . . . We're showing up for people who too many people view as disposable."[7]

Treatment

Inpatient Rehabilitation: There are a wide range of treatment options. Let's review some of the basics. Residential treatment programs offering medical supervision, counseling, and support. Often in a home-like yet therapeutic environment, inpatient or residential treatment offers a safe place for someone to leave the environment where their substance use disorder often took root. This is an excellent place to start, yet things like cost—especially for those without insurance—can be a barrier.

Outpatient Programs: Treatment allowing individuals to receive care while living at home is another option. This may be a cost-effective way to access support and treatment but still maintain employment, parent, go to school, or participate in normal activities. Outpatient treatment can span from intensive outpatient or high-intensity outpatient (usually around four hours per day) to medically managed outpatient.[8] This may be a good option for earlier-stage substance use disorder, with high-intensity outpatient more appropriate for severe SUD when inpatient or residential treatment is not an option. It is recommended that a mental health provider or substance use assessments like the American Society of Addiction Medicine criteria determine the best course of treatment and appropriate level of care for your loved one.[9]

Medication-Assisted Treatment (MAT): The use of medications like methadone and buprenorphine to treat opioid use disorder is a type of treatment. Some MATs like MOUD can have stigma attached to their use, especially in some settings like recovery housing. Many view the use of medication in stigmatizing ways, but it is helpful to remember that MAT, like any medication used to treat a condition like diabetes or depression, can be helpful.*

---

* For more information on where to find treatment options, check out "Resources for Families." Recovery.com is also an excellent resource and free online tool to help find individualized treatment for yourself or a loved one.

Recovery Support Services

Peer Support Groups: This type of recovery support service involves any type of support that involves people with lived experience in recovery. Meetings like AA, NA, any *A*, Celebrate Recovery, Recovery Church, All Recovery Meetings, Recovery Coaching groups, and other examples provide shared experiences and mutual support. Generally, peer support is centered on a shared life experience of having lived through addiction and into recovery. There are also family peer recovery supports that involve affected family members who are providing peer support to others.

Recovery Housing: This type of service is a safe living environment that promotes abstinence but is also inclusive regarding the use of medications for addiction treatment (e.g., MOUD) and to support long-term recovery. States in the US are moving toward greater regulations and standards for best practices in housing since many nefarious groups and individuals have started homes without accountability or experience. The National Alliance for Recovery Residences is a group that provides not only best practices but also tools for recovery home operators and developers. Organizations like Oxford House have also proven an evidence base for support, showing that those who live in recovery housing have a greater likelihood of success.

Recovery Community Organizations or RCOs: Furthermore, there are nonprofit and community-based organizations that offer services, education, and outreach to support recovery. RCOs (we do love our acronyms in recovery advocacy) help people in or seeking recovery (people like me) get plugged in to not only supportive services but also ways to give back and have purpose.

Sustained Recovery Approaches

Vocational Training and Continued Education: You may not consider employment or educational opportunities as part of a pathway of recovery, but these are key. Having a growth mind-set and learning that we have purpose in recovery (outside of just recovery itself) can be an integral part of sustaining long-term recovery. Anecdotally, I'd say that nearly 100 percent of the people I've met in sustained (what is sometimes referred to as "long-term") recovery have discovered new passion and grown either by going back to school, getting other types of vocational training, or working in a helping profession.

Volunteerism and Giving Back: Along with increased training and education, what does not take a college degree or a new certificate is having regular ways to give back to the community or volunteer. This could be through ministry or volunteer spots working with local community organizations, schools, or other services. Any opportunity to get outside of our heads (as a dear mentor of mine told me early on in recovery) can save our lives. Doing something for someone else reinforces the idea, again, that our lives have purpose and value. It is truly incredible how when we have other reasons to stay sober or maintain recovery (other than ourselves), this can reinforce the truth that we are a part of something bigger. Our lives matter and our sobriety matters because when we are clearheaded, we can show up in the ways that our communities and often families need.

Relationship and Life Skills: Last but not least (and remember this is a short list—the pathways of recovery are made up of innumerable pieces like a beautiful mosaic), my friends who have entered and maintained a sustained recovery do so by investing in improving their relationship and life skills. Assertive communication, honesty, empathy, boundaries, and other relationship skills can help us to repair and build healthy relationships in recovery. Having healthy connections with other human beings will create a stronger and healthier network of support—something that is central to a long-term recovery. Life skills, similarly, need to be built and practiced. Just like we aren't born knowing how to build credit or shop for and cook healthy meals, we need to learn the everyday life skills that will help us too.

As you can see, there are innumerable pathways of recovery; what I've shared are just a few examples. Note that almost none of them have to do with merely stopping drug or alcohol use.

Recommended Reading

Jennie Allen, *Get Out of Your Head: Stopping the Spiral of Toxic Thoughts* (WaterBrook, 2020).

Caroline Beidler, *Downstairs Church: Finding Hope in the Grit of Addiction and Trauma Recovery* (Morgan James Faith, 2023).

Caroline Beidler, *You Are Not Your Trauma: Uproot Unhealthy Patterns, Heal the Family Tree* (Lake Drive Books, 2024).

Henry Cloud and John Townsend, *Boundaries: When to Say Yes, How to Say No to Take Control of Your Life, Updated and Expanded Edition* (Zondervan, 2017).

Toni Collier, *Don't Try This Alone: How to Build Deep Community When You Want to Hide From Your Pain* (Nelson Books, 2025).

Jeffrey Foote, Carrie Wilkens, Nicole Kosanke, and Stephanie Higgs, *Beyond Addiction: How Science and Kindness Help People Change, Updated and Expanded Edition* (Scribner, 2014).

Pamela Lanhart, *Praying Our Loved One Home: Prayers of Hope for Prodigals Struggling with Addictions or Rebellion* (Pamela Lanhart, 2019).

National Institute on Alcohol Abuse and Alcoholism, "Neuroscience: The Brain in Addiction and Recovery," National Institutes of Health, last revised May 8, 2025, https://www.niaaa.nih.gov/health-professionals-communities/core-resource-on-alcohol/neuroscience-brain-addiction-and-recovery.

National Institute on Drug Abuse, "Drugs, Brains, and Behavior: The Science of Addiction," National Institutes of Health, July 2020, www.drugabuse.gov/publications/drugs-brains-behavior-science-addiction.

Recovery.com, www.recovery.com/resources/.

Resources for Families

Drug & Alcohol Family Support (DAFS): DAFS was created by two affected mothers to help support families and reduce the stigma of addiction and recovery. It provides peer support and other helpful resources for families in the UK. Website: https://www.dafsmk.co.uk.

Family Recovery Course (FRC): Be a Part of the Conversation is a nonprofit organization based in southeastern Pennsylvania. They have developed a helpful three-part course for affected family members that includes peer-led training on the complexity of addiction, the family component of SUD, and ways to build a recovery plan that supports the whole family system. Website: www.conversation.zone/frcdec3z/.

Mobilize Recovery: Mobilize Recovery is a national movement and annual initiative that brings together people in recovery, their families, and recovery advocates to create community-driven solutions to the addiction crisis. Website: https://www.mobilizerecovery.org/.

Partnership to End Addiction: This website has several different resources, including English and Spanish hotlines where trained professionals walk you through step-by-step ways to support your child or other loved one. They are available via text, email, or you can schedule a call. Website: www.drugfree.org/article/helpline-get-one-on-one-help/.

Recovery.com: This online platform is dedicated to helping individuals find local addiction recovery centers and explore various treatment resources and options. It offers guidance on starting the recovery journey, supporting loved ones, and addressing financial concerns related to treatment. Website: https://recovery.com/.

Thrive! Family Recovery Resources: This nonprofit organization provides hope and restoration to families affected by substance use or co-occurring disorders. They offer resources, support groups, education, advocacy, and healing connections grounded in compassion and understanding. Website: https://www.thrivefrr.org/.

Together Family Recovery: This organization creates space for healing and connection for families impacted by addiction and mental health challenges. Through powerful storytelling—including their featured documentary *Together Family Recovery*—they offer resources, education, and hope. Their mission is to break the silence around family pain and to empower loved ones with compassionate support and tools for lasting recovery. Website: https://www.togetherfamilyrecovery.com/watch-the-film.

Women's Recovery Leadership Foundation: Women's Recovery Leadership Foundation exists to ignite change by equipping women leaders in recovery with the tools, training, and community they need to thrive. Through bold advocacy, transformative education, and a focus on lived experience, this organization empowers women to lead with purpose and break cycles of addiction and trauma. Their mission is simple but powerful: to amplify the voices of women in recovery and create pathways to leadership that transform lives, families, and communities. Website: https://womensrecoveryleadership.com.

For a free family recovery plan resource, visit https://whenyoulovesomeoneinrecovery.com/.

Before You Go . . .

When we love someone in recovery, we can . . .

- Remember that our actions—healthy actions—can rewire our brain.
- Look at the similarities and not the differences.
- Remember that our loved ones are writing a new story.
- Recognize that change can happen, one conversation at a time.
- Enhance our understanding about what recovery is and change the way we think about it.
- Choose love first, no matter what road our loved ones are on.
- Remember that our limitations are gifts, and our need for boundaries is a treasure of the journey.
- Recognize that hope is not just a feeling; it is a strategy to help support your loved one.
- Remember that purpose is central to living a life of sustained recovery.

Recovery is about more than treatment for the *use* of substances. It is about *change* and enhancing a quality of life that makes us want to stay *in recovery* with purpose.

Acknowledgments

Dear reader, my first thank you is to you. This might not be an easy read for you, or perhaps you found your way here because it's been a rough road. I feel you. I wish I could grab a cup of coffee with you and listen to your story. No doubt, though the details may differ, we've experienced some of the same things and gone through some of the same trials: grief, sadness, fear, exhaustion, despair. And perhaps, there is also a shared joy, hope, gladness, and expectation. However you are showing up today, thank you for being here and for not giving up.

To my writing community and circle of support: I've learned over the years that as in life and recovery, so in writing. With every new book, I'm honored as the circle widens. To the Christian recovery writers' group: Jon, Christy, Jenn, Lee, Heather, Laura, Ericka, Zoe, Christina, Lisa, Em, Blake, and more, thank you for being trusted community. A special thanks to Jon Seidl for his invaluable feedback and thoughtful critique that led to me being more bold where it was needed. And thanks to Dr. Lee Warren for his expert review and input on the neuroscience presented in this book. To Darlene Brock, thank you for mentorship and sharing your wisdom. The Grit and Grace Project sisterhood has changed my life and my writing for the better.

To other trusted guides in publishing and writing: Brigitta Nortker, thank you for believing in this book from the beginning and your steady support. Your brilliant editing and vision have made this book so much more helpful for readers. It is an honor to partner with you! Trinity McFadden, thank you for your trust and for introducing this book to the amazing team at Nelson Books (Andrew Stoddard, Natalie Nyquist, Kristen Golden, Claire Drake, Devin Duke, Amanda Mae Steele, and Wesley Jakacki), who have stewarded this message with such confidence and zeal. Mike Salisbury from Yates and Yates Author Coaching, for your insight, guidance, and encouragement to keep going. Will Parker Anderson from the Writers Circle for helping me think about the craft of writing in new ways through your weekly newsletter and coaching. Mike Ruman from Local Growth for helping me to think bigger in terms of impact. Chloe Redfield for being the best marketing and brand manager an author could ask for. Cassie Baker for your marketing insights, belief in this mission, and podcast producing. Chloe and Cassie, your talent and creativity shine through in all you do.

A special thank-you to Clint Mally, Jeremiah Calvino, Josue Valadez, Kathryn West, Jennifer Zeidler, and the rest of the amazing team at Recovery.com. Your support of this book (and me) is incredible. This message would not have the same impact without you.

To my recovery family all over the world, thank you for keeping it real (and encouraging me to do the same). To my husband, Matt. Writing books is a dream that would still be dormant if you had not said, "I believe in you." To the rest of my family, including my mom, dad, and Greg: Thank you for loving me no matter what. And to my sweet kids, Henrick and Violet. This book is here because of your question, "What is recovery?" I'm so grateful to God, who has brought us together to answer this one day at a time.

Notes

Chapter 1: Everyone Has a Story

1. "Recovery," Substance Abuse and Mental Health Services Administration (SAMHSA), accessed July 25, 2025, https://www.samhsa.gov/find-help/recovery.
2. Beverly Conyers, *Addict in the Family: Stories of Loss, Hope, and Recovery* (Hazelden Publishing, 2003), 269.
3. Global Family Recovery Alliance, accessed December 4, 2024, https://www.globalfamilyrecoveryalliance.com/.
4. Ryan Hampton, *American Fix: Inside the Opioid Addiction Crisis—and How to End It* (St. Martin's, 2018), 217.

Chapter 2: Neuroscience for Normies

1. Queensland Brain Institute, "Understanding the Brain: A Brief History," University of Queensland, accessed October 8, 2024, https://qbi.uq.edu.au/understanding-brain-brief-history.
2. NIDA, "Drugs and the Brain," National Institute on Drug Abuse, July 1, 2011, https://nida.nih.gov/publications/drugs-brains-behavior-science-addiction/drugs-brain.
3. NIDA, "Drugs and the Brain."
4. Lee Warren, email to the author, March 29, 2025.
5. Judith Grisel, *Never Enough: The Neuroscience and Experience of Addiction* (Doubleday, 2019), 32.
6. Andrew Newberg, *How God Changes Your Brain: Breakthrough Findings from a Leading Neuroscientist* (Random House, 2009), 104.
7. Lee Warren, "Getting Better," *Self-Brain Surgery with Dr. Lee Warren*, October 20, 2024, https://drleewarren.substack.com/p/getting-better.

8. William White, "Hijacked Brains & the Question of Social Stigma," *Chestnut Blogs*, September 30, 2013, https://www.chestnut.org/Blog/Posts/32/William-White/2013/9/Hijacked-Brains-the-Question-of-Social-Stigma/blog-post/.
9. "The Neuroscience of Addiction in Recovery," Recovery Research Institute, accessed December 1, 2025, https://www.recoveryanswers.org/recovery-101/brain-in-recovery/.
10. Brian M. Hicks et al., "Consequences of an Adolescent Onset and Persistent Course of Alcohol Dependence in Men: Adolescent Risk Factors and Adult Outcomes," *Alcoholism, Clinical and Experimental Research* 34, no. 5 (2010): 819–33, https://doi.org/10.1111/j.1530-0277.2010.01154.x.
11. Xiaowei Zou et al., "Regional Brain Volume Changes in Alcohol-Dependent Individuals During Short-Term and Long-Term Abstinence," *Alcoholism, Clinical and Experimental Research* 42, no. 6 (2018): 1062–72, https://doi.org/10.1111/acer.13757.
12. Grisel, *Never Enough*, 20.

Chapter 3: The Recovery Journey

1. Nady El-Guebaly, "The Meanings of Recovery From Addiction: Evolution and Promises," *Addiction Medicine* 6, no. 1 (2012), http://www.addictionday.ca/wp-content/uploads/2013/02/The-Meanings-of-Recovery-From-Addiction_Evolution-and-Promises.pdf?form=MG0AV3.
2. American Society of Addiction Medicine, public statement on the state of recovery by the board of directors, 1982, accessed January 31, 2011, archived at http://www.asam.org.
3. Robert Granfield and William Cloud, *Coming Clean: Overcoming Addiction Without Treatment* (NYU Press, 1999).
4. David W. Best, "Cultivating Recovery Capital," accessed July 25, 2025, https://www.cultivatingrecoverycapital.com/.
5. Best, "Cultivating Recovery Capital."
6. William L. White and William Cloud, "Recovery Capital: A Primer for Addictions Professionals," *Counselor* 9, no. 5 (2008): 22–27,

http://www.naadac.org/assets/1959/whitewlcloudw2008_recovery_capital_a_primer.pdf.

7. Best, "Cultivating Recovery Capital."
8. Christi Hildebran, "Recovery Capital: Building Blocks for Sustained Recovery," *Comagine Health*, September 10, 2024, https://comagine.org/article/recovery-capital-building-blocks-sustained-recovery.

Chapter 4: Supporting Does Not Mean Enabling

1. Jeff Foote, Carrie Wilkins, and Nicole Kosanke, "The Craft Approach: Encouraging Healthy, Constructive, Positive Changes for Your Family," Partnership to End Addiction, last updated January 2025, www.drugfree.org/article/craft-community-reinforcement-family-training/?25519.
2. Jennie Allen, *Get Out of Your Head: Stopping the Spiral of Toxic Thoughts* (Waterbrook, 2020), 10.
3. Jeffrey Foote et al., *Beyond Addiction: How Science and Kindness Help People Change* (Scribner, 2014), 3.
4. John F. Kelly and Corrie Vilsaint, "Millions of Americans in United States Report Recovery from Substance Use Problem," Recovery Research Institute, July 20, 2020, https://www.recoveryanswers.org/research-post/millions-americans-in-united-states-report-recovery-from-substance-use-problem/.
5. Deborah Becker, "This Family Didn't Wait for 'Rock Bottom' to Help a Loved One with Their Addiction," WVPE 88.1, January 2, 2024, https://www.wvpe.org/2024-01-02/this-family-didnt-wait-for-rock-bottom-to-help-a-loved-one-with-their-addiction.
6. *Merriam-Webster.com Dictionary*, "Enabling," accessed January 4, 2025, https://www.merriam-webster.com/dictionary/enabling.
7. Beverly Conyers, *Addict in the Family: Stories of Loss, Hope, and Recovery* (Hazelden Publishing, 2003), 63.
8. Conyers, *Addict in the Family*, ix.
9. John Eldredge, *Resilient: Restoring Your Weary Soul in These Turbulent Times* (Nelson Books, 2022), 9.

10. "About Us: Hope Research Center," University of Oklahoma-Tulsa, accessed July 25, 2025, https://www.ou.edu/tulsa/hope/about.
11. Ricardo T. Muñoz et al., "Adverse Childhood Experiences and Posttraumatic Stress as an Antecedent of Anxiety and Lower Hope," *Traumatology* 24, no. 3 (2018): 209–18, https://doi.org/10.1037/trm0000149.
12. "Hope Research Center," University of Oklahoma-Tulsa, accessed July 25, 2025, https://www.ou.edu/tulsa/hope.
13. Brian J. Grim and Melissa E. Grim, "Belief, Behavior, and Belonging: How Faith Is Indispensable in Preventing and Recovering from Substance Abuse," *Journal of Religion and Health* 58, no. 5 (2019): 1713–50, https://doi.org/10.1007/s10943-019-00876-w.
14. Caroline Beidler, "Q: From a Mother Who Lost a Child," *Circle of Chairs*, October 24, 2024, https://carolinebeidler.substack.com/p/q-from-a-mother-who-lost-a-child/comments.
15. Pam Lanhart, *The Family Recovery Documentary*, Together: Family Recovery, accessed July 25, 2025, https://www.togetherfamilyrecovery.com/.

Chapter 5: Letting Go of Labels

1. Julie Merberg, "The Stories We Tell," *The Opposite of Addiction*, November 27, 2024, https://theoppositeofaddiction.substack.com/p/the-stories-we-tell.
2. Ryan Hampton, *American Fix: Inside the Opioid Addiction Crisis—and How to End It* (St. Martin's, 2018).
3. Lawrence H. Yang et al., "Stigma and Substance Use Disorders: An International Phenomenon," *Current Opinion in Psychiatry* 30, no. 5 (2017): 378–88, https://doi.org/10.1097/yco.0000000000000351; Nora D. Volkow, "Stigma and the Toll of Addiction," *New England Journal of Medicine* 382, no. 14 (2020): 1289–90, https://doi.org/10.1056/nejmp1917360.
4. "Stigma of Addiction in Mothers: Breaking Barriers," Mothers Against Addiction, September 8, 2024, www.mothersagainstaddiction.org/stigma-of-addiction-in-mothers/.

5. "About Family Coaching," Family Addiction Recovery, accessed July 25, 2025, https://www.familyaddictionrecovery.net/my-story.html.
6. Brennan Manning, *All Is Grace: A Ragamuffin Memoir* (David C. Cook, 2011), 194.
7. John 8:7, author's paraphrase.
8. Hosanna Wong, *You Are More Than You've Been Told: Unlock a Fresh Way to Live Through the Rhythms of Jesus* (Thomas Nelson, 2023).
9. "Stories," UNSHAME Kentucky, accessed November 10, 2024, www.unshameky.org/pages/story-library.
10. "Jason's Research on Leadership Traits of People with Addiction," UNSHAME Kentucky, updated October 25, 2024, YouTube, 1 min., 45 sec., https://www.unshameky.org/post/jason-s-research-on-leadership-traits-of-people-with-addiction.
11. National Institute on Drug Abuse, "Words Matter: Terms to Use and Avoid When Talking About Addiction," NIDA, January 2020, https://nida.nih.gov/sites/default/files/nidamed_words_matter_terms.pdf.

Chapter 6: Meaning in a Shared Story

1. Ryan Hampton, *American Fix: Inside the Opioid Addiction Crisis—and How to End It* (St. Martin's, 2018), 174.
2. Hampton, *American Fix*, 176–77.
3. William Stauffer, "Billstaufferpa," *Recovery Review*, accessed November 7, 2024, https://recoveryreview.blog/author/billstaufferpa/.
4. Robert H. Rice, "Narrative Therapy," *The Sage Encyclopedia of Theory in Counseling and Psychology* 2 (2015): 695–700, http://dx.doi.org/10.4135/9781483346502.n250.
5. Meghann Perry, Women for Sobriety Conference, June 2024.
6. "Types of Therapy: Narrative Therapy," *Psychology Today*, October 13, 2022, www.psychologytoday.com/us/therapy-types/narrative-therapy.
7. Anne Lamott, *Somehow: Thoughts on Love* (Riverhead Press, 2024), 155.

Chapter 7: Beyond Sober

1. Ian Lecklitner, "Climbing the Himalayas Helped Me Stay Sober," *The Phoenix*, January 8, 2025, https://thephoenix.org/resources/climbing-the-himalayas-helped-me-stay-sober--scott-strode-feared-an-overdose-would-end-his-lifeuntil-an-ice-climbing-brochure-put-him-on-a-new-path.
2. Ian Lecklitner, "Climbing the Himalayas Helped Me Stay Sober," *Men's Health*, January 14, 2025, https://www.menshealth.com/health/a63161776/climbing-the-himalayas-helped-me-stay-sober/.
3. "Bible Verses About Running," Bible Study Tools, accessed January 16, 2025, https://www.biblestudytools.com/topical-verses/bible-verses-about-running. All Scripture quotes taken from the ESV.
4. "History of Running," Ancientpedia, accessed January 16, 2025, https://ancientpedia.com/history-of-running/?form=MG0AV3.
5. Yannis Theodorakis, Mary Hassandra, and Fotis Panagiotounis, "Enhancing Substance Use Disorder Recovery Through Integrated Physical Activity and Behavioral Interventions: A Comprehensive Approach to Treatment and Prevention," *Brain Sciences* 14, no. 6 (2024): 534, https://doi.org/10.3390/brainsci14060534.
6. Dongshi Wang et al., "Impact of Physical Exercise on Substance Use Disorders: A Meta-Analysis" *PLoS ONE* 9, no. 10 (2014): e110728, https://doi.org/10.1371/journal.pone.0110728.
7. Magdalena Kukla-Bartoszek and Katarzyna Glombik, "Train and Reprogram Your Brain: Effects of Physical Exercise at Different Stages of Life on Brain Functions Saved in Epigenetic Modifications," *International Journal of Molecular Sciences* 25, no. 22 (2024): 12043, https://doi.org/10.3390/ijms252212043.
8. Margaret M. Hansen et al., "Shinrin-Yoku (Forest Bathing) and Nature Therapy: A State-of-the-Art Review," *Environmental Health and Preventive Medicine* 22, no. 1 (2017): 3, https://environhealthprevmed.biomedcentral.com/articles/10.1186/s12199-019-0822-8.
9. Jeffrey Foote et al., *Beyond Addiction: How Science and Kindness Help People Change* (Scribner, 2014), 5.
10. Lecklitner, "Climbing the Himalayas Helped Me Stay Sober."

11. Lecklitner, "Climbing the Himalayas Helped Me Stay Sober."

Chapter 8: Mental Health Is the Key

1. Portions of this section are quoted from Caroline Beidler, *When Anxiety Won't Let Go: Spiritual Meditation Practices to Ground You and Heal Anxiety and Panic Attacks* (Smart Living in Small Bites Series, 2024).
2. "Anxiety Disorders—Facts & Statistics," Anxiety and Depression Association of America, accessed July 25, 2025, https://adaa.org/understanding-anxiety/facts-statistics.
3. "Latest Federal Data Show That Young People Are More Likely Than Older Adults to Be Experiencing Symptoms of Anxiety or Depression," KFF, March 20, 2023, https://www.kff.org/mental-health/press-release/latest-federal-data-show-that-young-people-are-more-likely-than-older-adults-to-be-experiencing-symptoms-of-anxiety-or-depression/.
4. "Anxiety Disorders," Office on Women's Health, February 3, 2025, https://www.womenshealth.gov/mental-health/mental-health-conditions/anxiety-disorders.
5. "Facts and Statistics About Anxiety Disorders," CHC Resource Library, April 5, 2022, https://www.chconline.org/resourcelibrary/facts-and-statistics-about-anxiety-disorders/.
6. Caroline Beidler, "Anxiety and Depression and Other Rocks We Can't Drop," *Circle of Chairs*, November 9, 2024, https://carolinebeidler.substack.com/p/anxiety-and-depression-and-other.
7. Malasri Chaudhery-Malgeri, email to the author, March 29, 2025.
8. Chaudhery-Malgeri, personal communications.
9. Alicia Paul, "Bible Verses About Renewing Your Mind," Prayerlit, accessed January 30, 2025, https://prayerlit.com/bible-verses-about-renewing-your-mind/.
10. 2 Corinthians 12:5.
11. Jeffrey Foote et al., *Beyond Addiction: How Science and Kindness Help People Change* (Scribner, 2014), 10.

12. Jennie Allen, *Untangle Your Emotions: Naming What You Feel and Knowing What to Do About It* (Waterbrook, 2024), 7.
13. Caroline Beidler, "When That Feeling Feels Tough," *Circle of Chairs*, April 26, 2023, https://carolinebeidler.substack.com/p/when-that-feeling-feels-tough.
14. Adapted from Caroline Beidler, "How to Feel Emotions in Recovery Without Losing Your Mind," In The Rooms, October 30, 2022, www.intherooms.com/home/iloverecovery/addiction/how-to-feel-emotions-in-recovery-without-losing-your-mind/.
15. Fred Rogers Productions, "He Helped Us With Our Feelings," Mister Rogers' Neighborhood, accessed August 23, 2025, https://www.misterrogers.org/articles/he-helped-us-with-our-feelings/.

Chapter 9: Boundaries Are Brave

1. Malasri Chaudhery-Malgeri, personal communications, March 29, 2025.
2. Henry Cloud and John Townsend, *Boundaries: When to Say Yes, How to Say No to Take Control of Your Life* (Zondervan, 1992), 31.
3. Cloud and Townsend, *Boundaries*, 75.
4. Cloud and Townsend, *Boundaries*, 77.
5. Cloud and Townsend, *Boundaries*, 65.

Chapter 10: The Opposite of Addiction

1. Johann Hari, "Everything You Know About Addiction Is Wrong," TED Talk, London, June 2015, transcript, https://www.ted.com/talks/johann_hari_everything_you_think_you_know_about_addiction_is_wrong/.
2. Bruce K. Alexander, "Rat Park: How a Rat Paradise Changed the Narrative of Addiction," *Addiction* 114, no. 5 (2019): 917–22, https://doi.org/10.1111/add.14481.
3. Staff Writer, "There Are Ways to Fight Loneliness, Says Expert," Harvard T. H. Chan School of Public Health, November 8, 2023, https://hsph.harvard.edu/news/there-are-ways-to-fight-loneliness-says-expert/.

4. Kim Porter, interview with the author, October 24, 2024.
5. Stephanie Duncan Smith, *Even After Everything: The Spiritual Practice of Knowing the Risks and Loving Anyway* (Convergent, 2024), 20.
6. Substance Abuse and Mental Health Services Administration, "Value of Peers," 2017, PDF, https://www.samhsa.gov/sites/default/files/programs_campaigns/brss_tacs/peer-support-2017.pdf.
7. Garrett Moran, Hannah Knudsen, and Caroline Snyder, "Psychosocial Supports in Medication-Assisted Treatment: Recent Evidence and Current Practice," Office of the Assistant Secretary for Planning and Evaluation, July 7, 2019, https://aspe.hhs.gov/reports/psychosocial-supports-medication-assisted-treatment-recent-evidence-current-practice-0.
8. Valery Krupnik, "The Therapeutic Alliance as Active Inference: The Role of Trust and Self-Efficacy," *Journal of Contemporary Psychotherapy* 53 (2023): 207–15, https://doi.org/10.1007/s10879-022-09576-1.
9. Henri J. M. Nouwen, *The Wounded Healer: Ministry in Contemporary Society* (Image Books, 1979), 100.
10. 2 Corinthians 1:3–5.

Chapter 11: Healing Takes Time

1. Christina Dent, *Curious: A Foster Mom's Discovery of an Unexpected Solution to Drugs and Addiction* (Throne Publishing Group, 2023), 177.
2. Alcoholics Anonymous, *Alcoholics Anonymous: The Story of How Many Thousands of Men and Women Have Recovered from Alcoholism*, 4th ed. (Alcoholics Anonymous World Services, 2001), 164.
3. Jeffrey Foote et al., *Beyond Addiction: How Science and Kindness Help People Change* (Scribner, 2014), 96.
4. Steven M. Melemis, "Relapse Prevention and the Five Rules of Recovery," *Yale Journal of Biology and Medicine* 88, no. 3 (2015): 325–32, https://pubmed.ncbi.nlm.nih.gov/26339217/.
5. Foote et al., *Beyond Addiction*, 60.
6. Stephanie Duncan Smith, *Even After Everything: The Spiritual Practice of Knowing the Risks and Loving Anyway* (Convergent, 2024), 56.
7. Foote et al., *Beyond Addiction*, 17.

8. "The Serenity Prayer," *The Voice for Love*, The Voice for Love, https://thevoiceforlove.com/serenity-prayer.html.
9. Foote et al., *Beyond Addiction*, 17.

Chapter 12: Recovery Revival

1. L. A. Kaskutas, introduction to Marc Galanter and L. A. Kaskutas, eds., *What Is Alcoholics Anonymous?* (Oxford University Press, 2016), 253–59.
2. 1 Corinthians 5:17.
3. *Alcoholics Anonymous Comes of Age: A Brief History of A.A.* (Alcoholics Anonymous World Services, Inc., 1957), 199.
4. Ryan Holiday, *Stillness Is the Key* (Portfolio, 2019), 134.
5. Galanter and Kaskutas, eds., *What Is Alcoholics Anonymous?*, 118.
6. Galanter and Kaskutas, eds., *What Is Alcoholics Anonymous?*, 119.
7. Asia Ashraf, interview with the author, November 14, 2024.
8. Angela Fulton, "Finding Sobriety—and Jesus—in Vietnam's Christian Drug Rehabs," *Christianity Today*, November/December 2024, 42–51, https://www.christianitytoday.com/2024/11/vietnam-christian-drug-rehab-jesus-aquila/.
9. Fulton, "Finding Sobriety," 45.
10. Fulton, "Finding Sobriety," 42–51.
11. John Ortberg, *Steps: A Guide to Transforming Your Life When Willpower Isn't Enough* (Tyndale Refresh, 2025), 7.
12. Celebrate Recovery, *The 12 Steps and Their Biblical Comparisons*, PDF, accessed July 26, 2025, https://celebraterecovery.net/wp-content/uploads/12_steps_biblical_comparisons.pdf.
13. Ortberg, *Steps*, 23.
14. Brennan Manning, *The Wisdom of Tenderness: What Happens When God's Fierce Tenderness Transforms Our Lives* (Harper One, 2024), 50.
15. RPI Publishing, *The Twelve Steps—A Spiritual Journey: A Working Guide for Healing Based on Biblical Teachings* (RPI Publishing, 1994), 257.
16. Caroline Beidler, "When 'Christian' Is a Dirty Word," *Circle of Chairs*, July 1, 2023, https://carolinebeidler.substack.com/p/when-christian-is-a-dirty-word.

17. Mark Flynn, personal email to the author, February 10, 2025.

Chapter 13: Navigating Resources and Promoting Change

1. William Stauffer, interview with the author, November 7, 2024.
2. Stauffer, interview with the author.
3. Kayla Gill, "What Kind of Treatment Do I Need? Understanding Levels of Care for Addiction and Mental Health Treatment," Recovery.com, June 19, 2025, https://recovery.com/resources/what-kind-of-treatment-do-i-need/.
4. Jeffrey Foote et al., *Beyond Addiction: How Science and Kindness Help People Change* (Scribner, 2014), 5.
5. Tom Farley, email to the author, July 17, 2025.
6. Richard Rohr, *Essential Teachings on Love*, ed. Joelle Chase and Judy Traeger (Orbis Books, 2018), 12–13; 65–66.
7. Foote et al., *Beyond Addiction*, 51.
8. Foote et al., *Beyond Addiction*, 45.
9. Foote et al., *Beyond Addiction*, 69.

Chapter 14: Purpose Driven

1. Christina Dent, *Curious: A Foster Mom's Discovery of an Unexpected Solution to Drugs and Addiction* (Throne Publishing Group, 2023), 25.
2. Dent, *Curious*, 40.
3. Dent, *Curious*, 159.
4. Dent, *Curious*, 159.
5. Timothy Willard, "What Van Gogh and C. S. Lewis Teach," *The Beautiful Disruption*, April 4, 2024, https://timothywillard.substack.com/p/what-van-gogh-and-cs-lewis-teach.
6. Jeffrey Foote et al., *Beyond Addiction: How Science and Kindness Help People Change* (Scribner, 2014), 9.
7. Guilia Cambieri, "The Importance of Connections: Ways to Live a Longer, Healthier Life," Harvard T. H. Chan School of Public Health, December 8, 2024, https://hsph.harvard.edu/news/the-importance-of-connections-ways-to-live-a-longer-healthier-life.

8. Laura D. Kubzansky, Elissa S. Epel, and Richard J. Davidson, "Prosociality Should Be a Public Health Priority," *Nature Human Behavior* 7, nos. 2051–53 (2023), https://doi.org/10.1038/s41562-023-01717-3.

Chapter 15: Circle of Chairs

1. Valerie Forsey, personal communication with the author, 2024.
2. Valerie Forsey, interview with the author, November 8, 2024.
3. John Ortberg, *Steps: A Guide to Transforming Your Life When Willpower Isn't Enough* (Tyndale Refresh, 2025), 27.

Conclusion: Recovery Is for Everyone

1. Henri J. M. Nouwen, *Finding My Way Home: Pathways to Life and the Spirit* (Crossroad Publishing Company, 2001), 83.
2. Ryan Hampton, *American Fix: Inside the Opioid Addiction Crisis—and How to End It* (St. Martin's, 2018), 201.

Helpful Exercises

1. Jeffrey Foote et al., *Beyond Addiction: How Science and Kindness Help People Change* (Scribner, 2014), 67.
2. Elizabeth Bowen et al., "Development and Psychometric Properties of the Multidimensional Inventory of Recovery Capital (MIRC)," *Drug and Alcohol Dependence* 247 (2023): 109875, https://doi.org/10.1016/j.drugalcdep.2023.109875.

Recovery Pathways

1. "Preventing and Reducing Youth and Young Adult Substance Misuse: Schools, Students, Families," US Department of Education, last reviewed March 11, 2025, www.ed.gov/teaching-and-administration/safe-learning-environments/school-safety-and-security/preventing-and-reducing-youth-and-young-adult-substance-misuse-schools-students-families.
2. "3114: Engaging Youth in Drug Use Prevention," Global Coalition to

Address Synthetic Drug Threats, August 24, 2024, www.globalcoalition.us/node/160?form=MG0AV3.

3. "Families," Be Part of the Conversation, accessed July 25, 2025, www.conversation.zone/families/.
4. Substance Abuse and Mental Health Services Administration, "SBIRT: Screening, Brief Intervention, and Referral to Treatment," SAMHSA, last updated November 7, 2024, https://www.samhsa.gov/substance-use/treatment/sbirt.
5. "Recovery Friendly Workplace," Recovery Friendly Workplace, accessed July 25, 2025, www.recoveryfriendlyworkplace.com/.
6. Laura Sullivan, "A Look Inside the First Official Safe Injection Sites in U.S.," *PBS News*, March 9, 2022, https://www.pbs.org/newshour/health/a-look-inside-the-1st-official-safe-injection-sites-in-u-s.
7. Sullivan, "A Look Inside."
8. American Society of Addiction Medicine, "ASAM Criteria," accessed January 25, 2025, https://www.asam.org/asam-criteria.
9. American Society of Addiction Medicine, "ASAM Criteria."

About the Author

Caroline Beidler, MSW, is an author, speaker, and the managing editor of Recovery.com, an online resource that combines independent research with expert guidance on addiction and mental health treatment. Her own lived experience in addiction, mental health, and trauma recovery inspires her to help others find recovery in all its varying forms. She has built a global network of recovery supporters through her Substack newsletter, *Circle of Chairs*, which reaches thousands weekly. She is also a creative visionary and founded the Women's Recovery Leadership Foundation, which equips women in recovery to grow their impact, lead, and serve in their local communities. She also coleads a global research initiative on family recovery with leaders around the world. Her writing is described as funny, gritty, relatable, and insightful. Caroline lives with her husband and twins in East Tennessee, where she enjoys hiking in the mountains and building up her community's local recovery ministry.

Contact Caroline through her website:
https://www.carolinebeidler.com/